What People Are Saying About
Sell Like a Pro . . .

"*S*herrill Estes addresses some of the most challenging issues facing today's business people in *Sell Like a Pro* and her message is an important one; being successful these days is certainly no accident. Being ready to compete in the business world now means not only having the essential training and education, but also possessing the attitude and mental preparedness to work in an increasingly complex environment where there is a constant and steady stream of changing factors."

Martha Layne Collins
Governor of Kentucky
1983 – 1987

"*S*herrill has presented the basics of selling that focuses on understanding your customer and yourself. It's marketing at the front line. This book is for the newcomers planning on a sales career and an excellent reminder to those who have made it and who will continue to sell tomorrow's markets."

Carleton F. Rosenburgh
Vice President/Circulation
Gannett Newspaper Division
President, International Circulation Managers Association

"*Sell Like a Pro* is challenging, inspiring, and helps you to get the best from yourself. Excellent reading on how to be a champion in business or in one's daily life."

Coach Denny Crum
University of Louisville

"*Sell Like a Pro* is incredibly terrific, sharp, amusing, and interesting. Sherrill combines her style, sales savvy, and substance to make a great book."

Nido R. Qubein
Best Selling Author of *Get the Best from Yourself*
International Speakers Hall of Fame

"Sherrill's ideas on consultive selling are consistant with the realities of the marketplace; solid, down-to-earth approach. Sherrill has a practical pro-customer-oriented approach to help the new and experienced salesperson survive in today's competitive market."

Dave Mehl
Past President National Society Sales Training Executives
Manager of Sales Education Programs
General Electric Company

"*H*ere's an exciting plan that will show you how to turn your selling hours into gold."

Og Mandino
Author/Lecturer

"*E*very salesperson could benefit from Sherrill's book and seminars. Her solid advice, entertaining style, and common-sense approach to consultive selling have helped us achieve lasting sales results and build great customer relationships. A must for anyone seeking a receipe to success."

Kathy Schweitzer
Paragon Group

"*S*herrill has helped me set and achieve my goals, motivated me to be proactive in business and realize the importance of long-term successful customer relationships and repeat business. I recommend *Sell Like a Pro* as an excellent source for personal and professional learning and development."

Doug Johnson
Century 21
Hall, Powell & Roberts

"*S*herrill has the ability and knowledge to teach basics to beginners, while at the same time, she challenges the most seasoned professional with new and better skills and methods."

Jay Hall
Travelers Insurance Companies
J. W. Hall & Sons

"*T*he sense of each salesperson being perceived by the customer not just as a salesperson but rather as a consultant with information and solutions is a successful formula. This book is for the salesperson looking for insights toward developing consultive selling skills and would be extremely well-served by reading *Sell Like a Pro*."

Louis Filippo
Kinetic Presentations Inc.
President — Sales & Marketing Executives

"*S*herrill Estes says it all and more. Her combination of business acumen, integrity, and how-tos make this required reading for anyone who wants to achieve success. Anyone who wants to learn to sell his services, products, and ideas should study her philosophies."

Danny Thompson
American Suzuki Corporation of America

"*S*herrill's consultive approach to selling has helped me increase my new account and production numbers. But most important, her ideas have helped my repeat business in a 'bull market.'"

Carl F. Hyde
Account Executive/Financial Planner
Dean Witter Reynolds, Inc.

"*S*herrill Estes' sincerity is refreshing. She helps you make the most of your time, energy, and talents."

John Wright
State Farm Insurance Companies

Success Is Helping Others Succeed

"Sherrill is an expert salesperson. We gained fifteen years of knowledge in a two-day seminar!"

Don McFadden
Ford Motor Company

"An informative seminar that ensures successful customer relationships."

Faye Abramovitz
Ramada Inn

"Sherrill's dynamic personality and professional programs have been very effective in motivating our field managers and increasing their selling skills!"

Dave Thomas
Courier-Journal/USA Today

"Your seminar helped me to fine-tune my selling style and have greater confidence in selling my ideas."

Diane Seagle
Brown & Williamson Tobacco Company

"*S*herrill's consultation with
our corporate executives helped each of us position and
market our individual skills and unique talents and produce a
stronger organization."

Pepper English
South Central Bell

"*A* delightful and informative
presentation . . . we want more!"

Evelyn Mueller
National Association of Professional Saleswomen

"*S*herrill has been very effective
in helping our people to achieve immediate sales results."

John Ward
The Evening Herald

"*I* want to express my
appreciation for your excellent presentation. All of us were
challenged and motivated by your clear, well-organized
message. Thank you for sharing your insights on how to position
ourselves for success."

Bob Wade
National Speakers Association of Kentucky

"*S*herrill helped us become
successful in a competitive market."

Jack Haywood
PIP Printing

"*S*herrill's ideas are useful,
quickly absorbed, and highly effective for getting immediate results."

Roy Stinson
Thrifty Car & Truck Rental

"*I* found Sherrill to be very
stimulating and interesting. The skills I've learned from Sherrill
have greatly enhanced my career."

Paul Murphy
Boise Cascade

"*J*ust a brief note to
let you know how much your seminar was appreciated.
Sorry, we missed our monthly goal of $45,000
. . . we did $50,000 instead!"

Schuyler Ritter
Varngard Yabs, Inc.

Sell Like A Pro

Sell Like A Pro

The Secrets of Consultive Selling

Sherrill Y. Estes

ACROPOLIS BOOKS LTD.

WASHINGTON, D.C.

ACROPOLIS BOOKS, LTD.
Alphons J. Hackl, Publisher
Colortone Building, 2400 17th St., N.W.
Washington, D.C. 20009

Attention: Schools and Corporations
ACROPOLIS books are available at quantity discounts with bulk purchase for educational, business, or sales promotional use. For information, please write to: SPECIAL SALES DEPARTMENT, ACROPOLIS BOOKS, LTD., 2400 17th St., N.W., WASHINGTON, D.C. 20009.

Are there Acropolis books you want but cannot find in your local stores?
You can get any Acropolis book title in print. Simply send title and retail price. Be sure to add postage and handling: $2.25 for orders up to $15.00; $3.00 for orders from $15.01 to $30.00; $3.75 for orders from $30.01 to $100.00; $4.50 for orders over $100.00. District of Columbia residents add applicable sales tax. Enclose check or money order only, no cash please, to:

ACROPOLIS BOOKS LTD.
2400 17th St., N.W.
WASHINGTON, D.C. 20009

Library of Congress Cataloging-in-Publication Date
Estes, Sherrill, 1957-
   Sell like a pro.
   Includes bibliographical references and index.
   1. Selling.   2. Sales personnel— United States.
I. Title.
HF5438.25.E78 1988 658.8'5 88-16637
ISBN 0-87491-917-7

DEDICATION

To Chris
Thanks for your endless love, encouragement, sensitivity, and
belief in me.

To Ryan
The creative, loving, witty, charming, super sales kid who looks
like me.

FOREWORD

Like nearly every other aspect of our lives, doing business is not what is used to be. As we are thrust into a global economy, businesspeople recognize that we have to be ready to compete both domestically and internationally. None of us works in a vacuum; information is transmitted worldwide in the blink of an eye, and what may be state-of-the-art today is literally antiquated overnight.

Competition has always been a cornerstone of business, and being ready to compete in today's dynamic world means having the skills, training, education, and the ability to keep up a grueling pace that seems to quicken daily. Being ready to do business means something dramatically different than it did only a few years ago. Sherrill Estes shows us how to sell our unique advantages through expert positioning strategies.

In *Sell Like a Pro: The Secrets of Consultive Selling*, Sherrill Estes addresses these key issues, and her message is an important one: being successful today is certainly no accident. *Sell Like a Pro* will help you to build your business and create satisfied customers.

Sherrill Estes outlines a plan in these pages which will help you reshape your approach to how you do business. Sherrill's philosophy exphasizes three main points: position yourself to succeed; lock out competition through building long-term successful relationships with customers; and acquire the skills that allow you to compete successfully.

Interestingly enough, some of these same principles served me well during my years in public service. I hope you find your special formula for success in your business and enjoy this informative and relevant book.

> Martha Layne Collins
> Governor of Kentucky
> 1983-87

7

ACKNOWLEDGEMENTS

My heartfelt thanks to the hundreds of corporations and associations that have hired me to inspire, educate, and motivate their people.

Also, I am indebted to my family for "Motivating the Motivator" and for their understanding and support of my time away from them. Many thanks to the household help for taking care of "the boys" while I'm gone. A million thanks to Pam Johnson for her energy and creativity devoted to our projects.

Once in a while a wonderful friend and knowledgeable mentor comes along and gives his energy, talent, and time freely. But when that person happens to be considered the "guru" of the speaking industry, it becomes even more impressive. Thank you, Nido Qubein, for sharing your tremendous insights into the speaking industry and for your encouragement.

Finally, I would like to thank my colleagues at the National Speakers Association. However, my deepest appreciation goes to the thousands of individuals in my audience who believe in my message.

A SPECIAL WORD ABOUT
SHERRILL ESTES

As a successful businessman, I found *Sell Like A Pro: The Secrets of Consultive Selling* very attractive. Sherrill Estes has been selling all her life, early on as a child selling door-to-door greeting cards, and as an adult selling office equipment and financial services. Sherrill is accustomed to putting together big deals. She sold over $15 million in the financial industry in an eight-month period when she was only twenty-five years old. Today, as an entrepreneur, she speaks to more than 120 audiences a year across the United States, where she shares trendy ideas on the power of selling. Here's what you'll get out of this book.

Your positioning is what your clients and potential clients think and feel about you and your business. It's what they know and believe you can do for them—how well they understand and value what you are offering.

Your positioning is their confidence in your ability to do whatever you do with professional competence and expertise—how much they trust you to meet their needs. It is the way people feel about you and your business—how much they like the way you make them feel about doing business with you.

That's what this book is all about: It shows you that good positioning doesn't happen by accident. It is a result of a deliberate positioning strategy, backed up by a carefully conceived positioning plan, and consistent execution of that plan. In essence, that is what *Sell Like A Pro* is all about.

First, this book will help you to become pro-customer—to have a strong customer orientation. It suggests a new and deeper commitment to concerning ourselves first and foremost with the needs,

11

interests, and desires of the people we serve in every facet of our business.

Second, the book shows you how to become proactive instead of reactive. It helps all of us to make good things happen rather than only react to events as they are thrust upon us.

Third, this is a terrific work to help us to become committed to professional excellence in everything that we do. Sherrill Estes has been engaged for many years in the conceptualizing, designing, and executing of many sales development programs for large and small American corporations. She understands business from the inside out. Her sales savvy and business acumen go a long way to helping you understand the trends in the marketplace and how you too can be a master at selling.

> — Nido R. Qubein
> International Speakers Hall of Fame
> Author of *Get The Best From Yourself*

CONTENTS

Introduction

What is the difference between successful selling and success in general? Very little, if you ask me.

I've never known a successful person in general who didn't know how to sell, even if he or she claimed to have been unable to sell ice water to a desert traveler.

Let me explain what I mean. Success means a favorable result. Isn't that what a sale is? A transaction should offer a favorable result to both salesperson and customer. If either gets significantly more value than the other, the person holding the short end will refer later to the transaction as something decidedly less honorable than a sale.

A sale that results in mutual benefit is indeed a favorable result and, thus, an act of success in itself. By the same token, attaining success of any kind is an act of selling.

Every Successful Person Sells Something

Of course, not all successful people sell products or services. But they sell, nonetheless. The world is one big marketplace where skills, time, and talents are exchanged, or sold, for income. And no matter the profession, people won't be successful at anything until they sell themselves and others on their expertise. A person's success in any field—including professional sales—will be in direct proportion to the number and/or position of people who believe he or she is successful, or to the number and/or position of people he or she has sold.

Therefore, any successful person could become a good professional salesperson by learning the proper sales techniques. By the same token, the chances of success in any given field—particularly in professional sales—can be enhanced greatly by knowing the same selling techniques.

To put it simply, selling or success is taking something you believe in—whether it be a product, service, talent, skill, or point of view—and making others believe in it, too.

Dedicated to Professionals (Or Soon-to-Be Professionals)

I believe this book can be beneficial to anyone seeking any kind of success. I'm writing it primarily for the professional salesperson who wants to master the art and profit from it.

Unlike some other professions that offer low or, at best, limited incomes, selling can be as lucrative as you'd like. Some salespeople who are paid commissions have been known to draw higher incomes than the presidents of their companies. At twenty-five-years-old, I earned a six-figure income as a professional salesperson.

Yet, more than 90 percent of all people who undertake the profession of selling eventually get out of the business because they can't earn enough to survive!

If selling is so simple, why is it so tough? No matter how much you understand the concept behind selling, you won't go far in the field without knowing the techniques. And most sales failures don't know or use the proper techniques.

If you don't know the techniques, or if you feel that you could stand at least a good, solid review, then you're reading the right book.

Successful Salespeople Play by the Rules

Successful salespeople understand the power of selling. They try their best to make a sale, not only for the income it produces, but because they believe in their products. They know that neither they nor their customers will benefit if there is no sale. By the same token, they know that a fair sale offers satisfaction to both themselves and their customers.

Regardless of what you're selling, be it watches, widgets, or whatchamacallits, you too can keep your customers satisfied. Aside from knowing the proper techniques, it's mostly a matter of attitude that comes more or less naturally by being aware of long-term success. Long-term success comes from repeat business and satisfied clients. Instead of cold calls, we use direct mail and market ourselves as experts with solutions and ideas. We build our client base from a network of satisfied customers and by using expert positioning strategies. In short, we work smart instead of hard.

And that's the secret of success in sales. Although techniques are critically essential to any salesperson, equally important is knowing how to position yourself as an expert consultant in your line of sales. When you can do this, your buyers will be more than customers; they'll be clients who will buy from you time and time again.

This book, which will help you achieve expert positioning, is divided into four parts. The first section deals with the mental foundation that is essential for professional selling. It discusses the significance of selling like a pro, defines the ingredients of a successful sale, and details why professional salespeople must first sell themselves.

The second section is devoted to the significance of the buyer in any sales relationship. It offers advice on how to find new customers and how to keep them satisfied as well.

The third section of the book is devoted to the nitty gritty—the techniques themselves that make us salespeople successful. These include the art of probing questioning; offering facts, benefits, and evidence; cutting through stalls and overcoming objections; and tips on closing, or getting the okay for the order.

Finally, the fourth section of the book deals with practices that lead to sales success, including the setting of goals, time management skills, and the power of enthusiasm and a positive attitude.

Again, I contend that this book would benefit anyone who reads it, regardless of his or her profession, simply because a basic knowledge of sales won't hurt anyone living in a selling society. And that's exactly where we live, as I'll explain in the first chapter.

But for you, who are or would be professional salespeople, this book can be a ticket to a more productive, more profitable life.

Part I: Understanding Selling Today

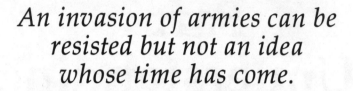

An invasion of armies can be resisted but not an idea whose time has come.

—Victor Hugo

1

The Impact of Selling Power on You

And the time has come to realize the power of selling in a selling society. Selling is the thread that holds a successful society together. No matter what a person does for a living, his or her job is related in some way to sales. Some people would be quick to challenge me on this by offering government employees and IRS agents as exceptions to the rule, but I'm equally quick to point out that they're mistaken.

People pay taxes to enjoy a free society. In effect, taxpayers are customers who have subscribed to police and fire protection, public instruction, garbage collection, and municipal services. People who work to support these systems are simply performing jobs that were promised in the sale. IRS agents, of course, are simply debt collectors who investigate customers who are suspected of being behind in their payments.

I challenge anyone to name any profession that isn't in some way related to or dependent upon sales. Manufacturers would go out of business without salespeople to move their products. Hospitals would go belly up if their services were given away instead of sold. Even ministers would have to find other jobs if churches didn't offer benefits to the congregation in exchange for donations.

As it has been said many times before, nothing happens in any business until something is sold. Consequently, John and Susie Q. Public—the typical American buyers—are bombarded constantly by a variety of sales messages.

How Many Can You Handle?

Think about it! How many sales messages do you receive during any given day? If you were to count them, you might be surprised.

For example, if you wake up to a clock radio to hear some fast-talking announcer squeeze as much selling as possible into a thirty-second time slot, you're hearing your first sales presentation of the day. After all, if it weren't for a sponsor, the announcer wouldn't have a show.

The same is true for television, of course. If you like to prepare for work while catching glimpses of some popular morning news-variety show (or any other show, for that matter), you'd best be prepared to see and hear at least several commercials.

When you're finished dressing and you sit down to breakfast, perhaps you'll look through the morning newspaper. Of course, it's full of advertisements, also. After all, it takes more than subscription fees to make a newspaper profitable.

As you finish reading your paper, you may notice several product containers that you or your family uses to prepare breakfast. Unless they're of the generic variety, which simply and solely states the name of the product, there probably will be a sales message printed on it. For example, "If it's Borden's, it's got to be good," or "Kellogg's Sugar Frosted Flakes are gr-r-reat!" If you don't believe it, take a stroll through a grocery store to see if most products aren't backed by a sales claim.

Off to work. Let's suppose you've had enough selling for one day already, so you choose to turn off the radio and ride in silence, effectively closing your ears to more sales messages.

Better close your eyes, too. Billboards abound, sporting various sales messages. Businesses display elaborate lighted signs publicizing their products and/or establishments. Even passing buses and taxicabs offer advertising space that is rented most often by someone who has something to sell.

By the time you get to work, you have received—or chosen to ignore—literally scores (if not hundreds) of sales messages. And the day has just begun. By the time it's over, there's no telling how many sales messages will come your way.

Wouldn't you agree that selling is pretty important? The power of selling is incredible. Having been a successful salesperson, I recognize the importance of selling. As an entrepreneur, selling seminars is my business. And if you too are to become very successful, you must learn how to sell correctly and profitably.

Thank Goodness for Modern Times

Long ago, when competition was scarce and consumers were more trusting, peddlers could make a lot of money by making heroic claims about their products. Of course, by the time customers discovered they had been taken advantage of, if not outright swindled, the peddlers had packed up their wares and were busy fleecing customers in the next county. Of course, some unscrupulous peddlers who didn't leave town discovered quickly enough what it was like to be tarred and feathered or run out of town on a rail.

Thank goodness, those days are gone (for trusting consumers as well as unscrupulous salespeople). However, the law of reaping what is sown is still in effect. Salespeople who are more interested in money than in satisfying their customers get their own just desserts in the form of bad reputations that will spread quickly among their customers.

We live in an age of information, and consumers are more savvy today than ever before. Competition today is stronger than it has ever been. Furthermore, the Federal Trade Commission's law that allows a consumer to back out of a contract within seventy-two hours after it is signed amounts to a swift kick in the pants to unscrupulous salespeople. They might make commissions in the beginning, but they'll starve in the end if they depend on sales for an income.

On the other hand, sensitive salespeople care more about customers than commissions or salary. It's not that they don't want money, but they don't want it at the expense of a successful long-term relationship. They want to take care of their customers, so their customers will continue to trust them to take care of their needs. A salesperson who practices this philosophy enthusiastically and energetically will find that money is the bountiful by-product of such a relationship. Several years ago, when I was selling business machines, I saw sales reps come and go. Why? Because of their careless attitude about their customers. Those of us who survived did so because we were sensitive to our customers' needs.

Many people ask me how I survived in the field of selling. Let me share an interesting story with you about my first day on the job. I, too, had assumptions about what a salesperson was supposed to be; aggressive and manipulative, know 101 ways to close a sale, answer a question with a question, and all the other things we'd been taught about selling. My first day on the job, my manager came to me and told me that the sales force would all appear in Evansville, Indiana, the next day for a blitz. As you may know, blitz is a term that was used in World War II. What we would all do is charge into someone else's territory and help him close deals using any technique we possibly could. So I rode with my sales manager to Evansville, we all gathered in a hotel for a session, and then were assigned our particular areas of town. Being the new person on the job, I was sent with another person to the Federal Building in Evansville. This particular building had a GSA (Government Services Administrator) who kept unsolicited visitors out of the building. Our job was to go door-to-door and drum up business. Within a few hours a GSA stopped us and asked what we were doing. We said, "We had an appointment to visit a person in the Veterans Administration to sell our dictaphones." This appeared to satisfy him for the moment and we continued to cold call and knock on doors. After another half-hour went by he caught up with us again. This time, we took off running down the fire escape and ended up outside. He was chasing us and yelling at us until we reached the door! Having run down several flights of stairs, I was totally out of breath and sick to my stomach. I thought I had to be crazy to be in this business! Although I had a strong sense of self-esteem and integrity, I felt that I wasn't aggressive enough to be successful in this career. Fortunately my natural sense of developing win-win relationships with customers and positioning myself for success, instead of knocking blindly on doors and making a lot of noise, is what really has enabled me to achieve great success as a consultive salesperson. I developed win-win relationships with my customers and I never resorted to manipulation. In turn, they introduced me into their world of associates and friends, where I had the opportunity to develop additional relationships.

What Makes the World Go Around?

You've heard it said that money makes the world go around. I'm sure it was said long before it was sung in the hit Broadway play and blockbuster motion picture, *Cabaret*. But I'll take minor issue with that statement. It isn't money as much as it is the desire to enjoy money that makes the world go around.

There are only a few different ways to get money. You can receive it as a gift, but unless you're the apple of some wealthy benefactor's eye, you won't get it often enough to pay your bills. You can inherit it, but that's no long-term answer for most people either. You can steal it, but that's the route to long-term imprisonment, not long-term success. The only other way to get it is to work for it. And remember, since all lines of work depend on selling, then somebody is going to have to sell something. And since you are a professional salesperson, you're it!

Yes, selling is what makes the world go around. And to illustrate my point further, let's discuss some nontraditional ways that people sell.

Selling in Disguise?

When the clock radio cuts on in the morning and the fast-talking announcer has completed the commercial, he or she might put on some music. Believe it or not, that's a sales message that resulted from a concerted effort. A recording artist, some back-up musicians, professional studio engineers, and a professional marketer are joining forces to sell a song. There's big money for all involved if the song catches on.

When you watch any television show, you're receiving another concerted sales message. Once, officials of any major commercial network had only two competitors. The "Big Three"—CBS, NBC, and ABC—pretty much had the television market sewn up. With the increase in cable stations, pay-movie services, and various UHF channels, competition abounds for programming. As a result, when you watch any given television show, you have been sold on the belief that the particular show you're watching is the best the set has to offer at that particular time. And it has been reported that when ratings go down on the "CBS Evening News," Dan Rather dons his "serious selling" sweater. Station officials must sell the programs so you can watch their sponsors' efforts to sell their products. Whew! As Jerry Lee Lewis might say, there's a "whole lot of selling going on."

Let's go back to the newspaper. The newspaper company is in the business of selling newspapers. Of course, the newspaper sells ads and subscriptions to raise revenue, but ads and subscriptions alone don't sell papers. The papers must have fresh, interesting news presented in a manner convenient to the readers so that they will buy this particular newspaper over many others available. This is accomplished by packaging the product as attractively as possible. The most important articles of the day are offered on the front page; news of lesser interest is printed on the inside pages. Offering headlines to catch the reader's eye and an encapsulated version of the story in the first couple of paragraphs, the newspaper sells the story to the reader. If the newspaper didn't sell news, people probably would start taking other newspapers, or they would depend solely on television news, which also sells stories through similar packaging. And after traveling the country presenting sales training seminars for newspaper employees, I know one of the major objections they hear is, "I get my news from the TV."

Now, for even less conventional means of selling. Turn to the editorial page, where you'll see columns written by people who are trying to sell you on their way of thinking. Whenever you see a band of people protesting or picketing, they are attempting to sell their beliefs to gain support for their cause. Acid rain, Star Wars, nuclear power plants, capital punishment, labor disputes, taxes, abortion, and surrogate motherhood are just a few of the hot sales topics of this era. Armed with a professional salesperson's passion, people on both sides of each issue do their best to sell their ways of thinking to others.

And if it's election time, hold on to your hats. Political candidates win and lose elections because they either have or don't have a sufficient selling effort behind them. Newspaper, billboard, radio, and television advertisements hawk a particular candidate, aided by bumper stickers, campaign signs, and door-to-door volunteers. In the end, the person who is picked for the position is the one who most successfully sold his or her point of view and image to the mainstream of voters.

Do teachers teach, or do they sell? Teachers can detail any given point to the nth degree. However, if the students don't retain the information, nothing has been taught. Successful teachers sell their lessons by making instruction interesting through illustrations and anecdotes. They find that their students will buy much more willingly than students of teachers who only talk.

Even the field of religion isn't safe from selling, and a lot of money changes hands in the process. A local minister tries to sell you on a particular way of thinking. Large amounts of money are collected regularly because someone sold religion to others. Whether the sellers are representatives of an established church or a questionable cult, the sales process applies. In fact, when you mix religion with television, you have grand-scale selling. Well-known television ministers draw tremendous salaries selling salvation to viewers who either aren't aware or don't care that money isn't required to obtain it. When it comes to selling, you can believe it: everything is sold.

As I said in the introduction, selling is nothing more than making others believe in what you believe, or value what you value, whether it's a song, a television show, a news story, a political position or candidate, a course of instruction, eternal salvation, or—last but not least—a product or a service.

Selling Success

Have you ever wondered what separates successful people from failures? Successful people are successful at selling. This is true for professional salespeople as well as people in other fields of endeavor.

Think about all of the successful people you've known. They became successful only after they were able to sell an image of success to enough of the right people. Again, as I said in the introduction, a person's success in any field—including professional sales—will be in direct proportion to the number and/or position of people who believe he or she is successful, or to the number and/or position of people he or she has sold.

As professional salespeople, such people are successful at selling their products. By knowing how to position themselves as experts in their market, they are able to get the commissions they want. As employees, they are successful at selling their abilities to their supervisors. By knowing the right skills, packaging themselves appropriately, and being able to interact positively with others, they are able to land the jobs they want. As spouses, they sell the prospect of life-long companionship. I have been married to the same man since I was seventeen and nowadays, that takes a lot of selling and servicing by both parties! Relationship selling is keeping the customer satisfied.

Everything you do is selling. Look at the way you dress. Aren't you selling something to someone? It's called image, and the clothing industry (not to mention virtually every other form of popular culture) thrives on images. Even people who pay no attention to the fashion experts are selling their individuality to others, if not themselves. Such was the case during late 1960s and early 1970s when the so-called freakish image of flannel shirts, faded jeans, and fringe jackets was so popular with youth of that era.

Look at your car. Aren't you selling something again? If you drive a Cadillac, Mercedes-Benz, BMW, or Rolls Royce, you're selling a successful image to others. If you drive an expensive sports car, you're selling a successful, free-spirited image. Even if you drive an economy car, there are many models from which to choose, and you undoubtedly chose the one that best suited your tastes; and that sells your image accordingly. Even if you drive a clunker, you're selling to all who see you that you live on modest means or that you don't care what they think about you or your car.

After years of selling greeting cards as a youngster, later selling office equipment and financial services, I know value is a perception. And perceptions become reality. Position yourself as a successful person, and you will become successful.

Successful people are successful because they sell successful images and are able to bring them to reality. Failures are unsuccessful because they can't or won't deliver the successful images they sold. In short, they looked good, behaved properly, and put their best foot forward during their job interviews, their dating and engagement periods, and their applications for long-term credit. But when it came time to deliver by employing good skills, contributing positively to their relationships, or making their monthly payments, they didn't deliver. That's one reason why jobs are lost, marriages fail, and merchandise is repossessed—because someone sold a successful image but didn't deliver.

It's not that these people couldn't sell; on the contrary, they were very good at it. They just didn't deliver, and a pro always delivers. Unscrupulous salespeople take the money and run.

And, of course, some people fail because they are unable or unwilling to sell a successful image at all. These include street people, some welfare recipients, virtually all criminals, chronic alcoholics and drug dependents, and a good portion of the people committed to mental institutions.

Even these people were selling something. Unfortunately for them, it was an image that no one else wanted to buy. They were salespeople who had nothing to offer to a selling society.

We do more than just live in a selling society. We are a selling society. We sell from the day we're born. Babies can't talk, but they let you know they're hungry or otherwise dissatisfied by crying. That's selling, because the parents who pay off with a fresh bottle or diaper are buying contentment for the babies and silence for themselves. As we grow, we continue to sell to get what we want, and we keep selling until the day we die.

Selling is serious business. In fact, selling is our only business. Bearing that in mind, we'd better do it right, or we will lose our international clout.

Successful Selling Is Keeping Promises

Good salesmanship is nothing more than making a promise you can keep, while poor salesmanship is defaulting on claims or making no claims at all. History has proven that products without sales claims—generic groceries, for example—have by and large disappeared from the American scene. Although they were considerably cheaper than their brand name counterparts, they were passed over to the point of virtual extinction. On the other hand, many generic drug companies have fared well by comparison. Why? Because generic drug companies are willing to claim that the drugs will perform as well or better than their brand-name counterparts.

People don't want to deal with products or other people who can't or won't state claims, and they'll stop dealing with people and products that can't live up to stated claims. To function in this selling society, a person or product must make a claim and live up to it. However, there is a great deal of difference between functioning and being successful. And successful salespeople are successful because they are no longer peddlers of products. They are experts with solutions and ideas. In short, they make and keep high promises.

In short, if you would be a successful salesperson, you only have to do what all successful people do. Simply stated, you must sell.

And by now, I hope you understand that you probably know more about selling than you realized. Think of every successful accomplishment you've performed thus far in your life. Think of how you were actually selling. When you can sell a product with the same energy that you used to accomplish your past successes, you'll be well on your way to the 10 percent of all professional salespeople who survive and prosper.

Like it or not, selling is something you'll be doing for the rest of your life—one way or the other. There's no way around it. So if you can't beat them—and you can't—then why not join them?

Join me, if you will, in the next chapter where we'll take a look at what constitutes a successful sale. The more familiar you are with the anatomy of successful transactions, the more adept you can become at arranging them.

Chapter in Review

1. Selling is the thread that holds a successful society together. No matter what a person does for a living, his or her job is related in some way to selling.

2. Selling is a field that will always have vacancies for people who are willing to do it correctly—and profitably.

3. Successful salespeople are sensitive. They care more about customers than commissions or salary.

4. Selling is nothing more than making others believe in what you believe in, or value what you value.

5. Selling is what separates successful people from failures, regardless of their fields of endeavor.

6. To function in this selling society, a person or product must make a claim and live up to it. Successful salespeople are successful because they make and keep high promises.

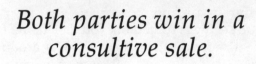

Both parties win in a consultive sale.

—Sherrill Estes

2

Winning with Consultive Selling

If selling is the thread that holds society together, the next question that comes to mind is, what makes a selling society tick?

I could answer that question by alluding to Abraham Maslow's hierarchy of human needs, which includes survival, security, belonging, ego gratification, and self-actualization. But such discussion would be a waste of space, because every time a deal is put together, the motivating factor is: "Let's do something together for the benefit of both of us."

That's what makes a selling society tick. I dare say that 100 percent of what people do for others is done to get rewards for themselves. Of course, some people do things for others just for the joy it brings. While that's certainly a nice and noble thing to do, the person who is so charitably motivated still enjoys the reward of personal joy. As they used to say in the '60s "If it feels good, do it."

In selling situations, however, the reward is usually something of at least equal tangible value. Manufacturers couldn't stay in business long if salespeople sold $100 products for $20 each. By the same token, consumers have their own financial books to balance, and consumers who regularly pay five times the going rate for products won't be consumers for long. Instead, they will be the consumees—they'll be eaten alive by debt and bankruptcy.

"Let's do something together for the benefit of both of us." This is a natural human desire that is expressed early in life. I see it when my son Ryan trades toys with his friends and when they do favors for each other. This natural desire stays with us as long as we live. It's the desire that allows us to grow and prosper.

So remember that whenever you're selling anything, be it tangible or intangible, your prospects must be aware of what's in it for them. Good salespeople don't beat around the bush; they make the benefits clear, and they make no claims that misrepresent what they are selling. They know that the best way to keep customers buying is to focus on what's in it for them.

Benefits Are Very Personal

For the most part, consumers aren't going to be taken in by outlandish claims. Thanks to stereotypical fast-talking hucksters, most consumers today are wary of salespeople who just can't say enough about their products. The more praise the salespeople heap on, the more suspicious the prospects become.

Consumers want to know how products and services will benefit not all consumers, but them in particular. After all, consumers come from various businesses, situations, and backgrounds. The benefit that makes a product or service vital to one person might well be of little value to another. Salespeople who insist on sticking to general claims and resist taking the time to learn about the prospect's individual needs are saying, in effect, that they are less concerned about their prospects than the money the sale stands to bring them.

That method might have worked in the past, but it's not the way to be successful in sales today.

Consultive Selling

Salespeople who succeed today and will succeed in the future are those who exhibit a different attitude altogether. They want to learn all they can about their prospects' desires. Successful salespeople know that a satisfied customer is good for not only one sale, but many future sales as well.

That's why successful salespeople won't run the risk of alienating their customers. They will determine before the sale that the prospect has the correct understanding about the product or service and that it can satisfy the prospect's individual needs.

This can be achieved only through meaningful consultation with the prospect—a give-and-take exchange of prospect needs and product claims. When prospects have an opportunity to explain their individual needs, the salesperson will be in the best position to recommend a product to serve them.

By using a consultive selling approach—and being concerned about the prospect—a salesperson will be in the best position to benefit the prospect.

Think about consultive selling when applied to a nontraditional mode of selling. Suppose you want to be a friend to someone. If, in the person's presence, all you can do is talk about yourself, it might be tough to form the friendship. On the other hand, if you take the consultive approach, you would prompt the other person to talk about himself or herself, and you would spend a considerable amount of time listening.

Any sales trainer worth his or her salt will tell you that the best way to get prospects to like you is to get them to talk about themselves. It's also the best way to get information about prospects that you can use later to help them make wise buying decisions.

True, salespeople in the past could sell by using virtually any approach. Competition was slim, and consumers were more naive than today. But salespeople who want to survive in the future had better develop a consultive selling style. When prospects realize you're more interested in making them happy than in making the sale, they'll trust you more and, consequently, will be more willing to buy from you. And when that happens, you'll be in a position to close sales faster and more often than most salespeople practicing today.

Three Ingredients of Consultive Selling

Of course, you must believe in your product and take care of your customer to be successful. But that's just the start. To be truly successful, you must be able to convince your prospects that you will stand behind them as well as your products. I can't tell you how to do that in one paragraph; I'll need the rest of the book.

In many years of successful selling, and teaching thousands of others how to sell, I've discovered that there are three basic ingredients of consultive selling.

1. *Product knowledge.* Develop an in-depth knowledge of the features and benefits of your product or service so that you can tailor your presentation to each individual's needs. Also, develop knowledge of any policies or information that can help you better service your customers and build trust and value into the relationship.

2. *Selling skills.* Actually, this is a matter of personal style. I call them conversational skills, because selling is a matter of conducting a sensitive conversation. With these skills, successful salespeople develop the ability to interview customers and recommend specific solutions for their individual problems. You must develop your own individual style, or you'll sound canned at best and phony at worst. *Get real!* Be creative in your approach to presenting your product. After all, few, if any, of your sales presentations will be alike.

3. *Attitude.* A salesperson will stay in business only as long as he or she has customers. And keeping good customers depends a lot on the salesperson's attitude. Successful salespeople adhere to the belief that a satisfied customer is a loyal customer. That's why service is the most important component of the consultive selling process. Poor service alienates customers, while ex-

cellent service satisfies them. Develop long-term, mutually satisfying relationships with your customers.

Of course, when it comes to the first ingredient, you're on your
own. But I'm sure your company will help you in that department. This book will help tremendously in building your selling
skills, which is the second ingredient. And, of course, I would be
remiss if I didn't suggest that you recommend Sherrill Estes for
your sales training. Move over, Lee Iacocca. I can ask for the order
in my book, too!

But development of the third ingredient is up to you. A salesperson in control of his or her attitude will not lose sight of the fact
that the customer's satisfaction comes first, because providing
good service is in the salesperson's best interests. I'll explain this
concept further in the next chapter.

Levels of Selling

Let's take a look at the various levels of selling to give you an idea
of the various types of sales that can materialize from any given client. Learn these levels to boost your sales' batting average.

1. *The Creative Call.*   This is the call you might make to a
   prospect who has never used your product or service
   and, in many cases, has never thought about using it.
   That doesn't necessarily mean the prospect is happy
   with his or her situation. It just means that he or she is
   not sufficiently unhappy to have taken the initiative to
   look into your product or service.
      With this type of prospect, you'll have to take it from
   square one. Telling this prospect about the capabilities
   and features of a computer won't score any points
   with him or her until you explain just how a computer
   could benefit his or her business. Perhaps your company's advertisements and promotions (or even those of
   your competitor) have aroused the prospect's curiosity
   somewhat, but they didn't do the complete job, or else

the prospect would have called you. So the first step of a creative call is to establish a need. In other words, you should enlighten the prospect. Make him or her aware of the problem that your product can solve.

2. *The Competitive Call.* Once the creative salesperson has made the prospect aware of the problem, the sale is fair game to anyone who can close it, be it the original salesperson or a competitor. It can be a real letdown to hear your prospects say they're going to ask for other bids. But by the same token, it can be a real surprise to sell a product to a customer who was introduced to it through another salesperson. Two can indeed play at the competitive selling game.

Suppose a salesperson makes several calls during the creative stage of the sales process, and these calls are devoted to selling the idea or establishing the problem. If and when the sale becomes competitive, the salesperson starts all over again. But let me say this: you need to know as much or more about the competition as you do about your own product or service. And after years in this business, it's rare that a deal doesn't get competitive. Develop a profile on each of your competitors' products or services, and try to sell your "exclusives." All levels of selling have the potential to become complicated by competition, and the salesperson must be alert and aware of all the possibilities. He or she must be well-organized and very skilled in the consultive selling process to succeed in the competitive game.

3. *The Retail Sale.* This is a sale that occurs when prospects discover all by themselves that they have problems. On the simplest level, this occurs when they run out of groceries, need new clothes, develop an illness for which they need medicine, and so on. As a result,

the prospect will call you, or even come to your place
of business.

4. *The Add-On Sale.*   This is selling to the customer who
   has already bought a product. For example, a customer
   who buys a new suit might be interested in a new pair
   of shoes, or at least a new shirt. The new car customer
   might be open to the possibility of adding a new stereo
   system to the car he or she has just ordered. This is
   sometimes called suggestive selling or related-item
   selling. Many sales situations present this opportunity,
   whether they are retail or creative sales. Generally, it's
   easier to make the second sale, once the customer's initial need is satisfied. It's also good business.

5. *The Upgrading Sale.*   This is similar to the add-on sale,
   except that it involves buying a better product instead
   of a second one. Most companies offer varying grades
   of products, ranging from good to better to best. Of
   course, when you sell a top-of-the-line product, all
   parties benefit. The customer gets better quality,
   longer life, and increased performance while the salesperson makes a larger sale. The company benefits
   from increased dollar volume, better profit structure,
   and reduced delivery costs.

6. *The Account or Service Sale.*   This is the transaction
   that occurs when a salesperson makes regular calls on
   established users or resellers of the company's products. In the beginning, this was a creative sale; a salesperson sold the user or merchant on the product. Now,
   the sale is somewhat like a retail sale, except that the
   salesperson comes to the customer's place of business.
   The account or service sale has excellent potential for
   add-on selling (expansion of product line) as well as
   for upgrading selling.

A major secret to success in selling or anything else is using your time wisely and having the good judgment and self-confidence to use your imagination. Realizing that there are only a finite number of hours we can work each day, I always look for short cuts and ways to simplify the systems I use. For example, I often use the telephone instead of sending out a lot of correspondence. However, my direct mail campaign, which I used in the financial industry, helped me sell over $2 million each month. Targeted mail was the key. One particular private school that taught students the trade of electronics had been receiving my direct mail and phone calls about a variety of investments. One morning, when I called the prospect, he said he wanted me to stop by and pick up some money to invest. When I visited with him he gave me $200,000 in cash to put in a six-month certificate of deposit. As I drove back to the office in my convertible with the $200,000 in large bills in my possession, I envisioned a life of lying on the beach for a while, even though I knew the money was going into the safe immediately. But, when I walked in and put the $200,000 down on the director's desk, he was stunned. He couldn't imagine a customer giving me such a large sum of money in cash. Although I often received $200,000 to invest for a client, none had ever given it to me in cash. Since this was his first investment with me, I too was surprised.

He continued to invest his money with me and I was able to persuade him to allow us to do the financing for his educational loans as well. It is through this kind of sensitivity and relationship building with your customers that you will be able to position yourself for success. I believe in penetrating your markets, but you can only do that through servicing your clients and by being aware of additional business opportunities. You must have the foresight in your business dealings with your customers to realize what their business means to you in the months and years to come.

As I mentioned, the account or service sale calls for sound judgment on the part of the salesperson. Here are some of the problems that can develop.

    a. *Overservice.* The salesperson gives the customer extra attention at first to ensure customer satisfaction. Then, it

gets to be a habit. It's easier on the nerves for a salesperson to call on an existing account than it is to make a creative call on a brand new prospect, who might turn
down the salesperson. Some salespeople get so wrapped
up in service accounts that they claim to be too busy to
make creative calls.

b. *Underservice.*   On the other hand, a salesperson who
takes a customer for granted and consequently fails to
provide sufficient service might well lose the account to
the competition. When that happens, the salesperson
uses the opposite of the overservice excuse. That is, he or
she is too busy making time-consuming creative calls to
provide good service to existing customers.

c. *Underselling.*   Salespeople often make sales, yet they
never stop to consider that the customer might be able to
use other products as well. A failure to add-on or up-
grade a sale makes the customer ripe for the competition.
It's a lot easier for the other guy to make such a sale,
since the first salesperson already has established the
value for the product.

d. *Overselling.*   Some salespeople, for example, load up
their accounts with more merchandise than is needed
and/or with grades that don't move well in the customer's market. Sure, this will keep the competitor away, but
the customer will likely learn to hate the salesperson
each time he or she sees the huge pile of dead stock or
realizes the restriction on his or her cash flow. Such
salespeople always come up with an excuse: "I've just got
to make quota; you know that sales manager of mine!"

To realize when he or she should or should not escalate a sale, a
salesperson must have judgment, which generally (like anything
else) improves with practice. Knowledge is important, too. When
company policy is violated in one of these areas, the salesperson
who says, "Gee, I didn't know," certainly sounds uninformed.

Of course, you can make good sales that will benefit both you
and your customer by knowing these various types of sales and

when to work toward them. Stay abreast of company policy and use good judgment when escalating your sales.

Benefit for Benefit

The world is full of fair-weather friends. Perhaps you've had a few yourself. They're the type of people who are easy to find when times are good. However, when a personal problem or misfortune develops, they're hard to find. They'll help you share your good times, but they'll have no part of your bad times. People like that are usually the first to go whenever you revise your friend list.

Unscrupulous salespeople are like fair-weather friends. They want your money very much, but they want no part of problems that may arise from your use of their products. As a result, they are the type of salespeople you'd like to strangle, if you ever get the chance to see them again.

A sale must be a benefit-for-benefit exchange between salesperson and buyer. If the scales are tipped in favor of either party, ill feelings will develop. Consultive salespeople work diligently to ensure that the scales are balanced from the start; they know that the best way to avoid problems later is not to allow any to occur. They also know that avoiding problems is the best way to build a relationship of trust.

Trust Doesn't Come Easy

Possibly because of the stereotypical salesperson's passion for quick commissions, prospects have become more wary of salespeople over the years. Trust is very important in the sales relationship. To give you an example, suppose you're watching television and an old movie comes on. If the movie opens with a logo from one of the popular motion picture studios, such as Warner Brothers, Universal, Twentieth-Century Fox, Metro-Goldwyn-Mayer, Paramount, or Columbia, then you have a pretty good idea that the movie might be good. After all, most of the motion picture classics have been produced by these studios.

At this point, the credits appear and list the stars in the movie, then the title, then the supporting cast. If you see the names of actors and actresses you recognize, you might decide to watch the movie, based on your trust of the studio and the actors and actresses involved.

On the other hand, if the logo reveals that the movie was produced by a studio you've never heard of, you might switch channels on that basis alone. If not, the credits or the first five minutes of the movie had better offer something to arouse your curiosity, or gain your trust that the movie will have some redeeming value.

The same is true with salespeople. If you represent a reputable firm such as IBM, Kodak, or AT&T, prospects' doors may swing open for you. Like the person trusting the established studio, prospects might trust you because of your affiliation with a reputable company.

However, if you work for a lesser-known company, the responsibility of building salesperson-client trust will fall into your lap.

It's not easy, but it's also not impossible. The next chapter will explain how it is done.

Chapter in Review

1. The motivating force behind a selling society can be summed up in one simple sentence: "If you'll do something for me, I'll do something for you."

2. Whenever you're selling anything, be it tangible or intangible, your prospects must be aware of what's in it for them.

3. Consumers don't want to know how products and services will benefit all consumers, but how products will benefit them in particular.

4. Successful salespeople consult with prospects to determine their needs, then recommend the product or

service that will best satisfy those needs. This is the consultive approach to selling.

5. The three ingredients of consultive selling are product knowledge, selling skills, and attitude. While a company can help with the first two, the development of attitude is up to the individual.

6. There are various levels of selling, including the creative call, the competitive call, the retail sale, the add-on sale, the upgrading sale, and the account or service sale.

7. A sale must be a benefit-for-benefit exchange between salesperson and buyer. If the scales are tipped in favor of either party, ill feelings will develop.

It is one of the most beautiful compensations of this life that no man can sincerely try to help another without helping himself.

—Ralph Waldo Emerson

3

Get Real and
Get the Business

Author Denis Waitley in his book, *Seeds of Greatness*, tells a story about the origin of the word sincere.

Long ago, in ancient Rome, sculptors were in great demand. It was extremely fashionable during that era for citizens to adorn their homes with statues of the gods. These statues were regarded as status symbols, much like modern day citizens judge their peers by the caliber of automobiles they own.

Of course, some sculptors weren't as highly skilled or principled as might be desired. Yet, they were often good at covering their blunders. Some sculptors could conceal statue flaws with wax so well that customers couldn't recognize the difference between inferior statues and those of high quality.

The highly skilled sculptors decided they had better take action, lest their unprincipled competitors take away their business. So they started posting signs with their works that read *sine cera*, or "without wax." When customers saw the *sine cera* sign, they knew they were looking at the real thing.

Every customer wants the real thing. Successful salespeople are sincere in their efforts to help the customer find it. Amateurs simply want to make the sale and get the money. But eventually they'll have to find other ways to get money, because amateurs generally fail at selling.

It's a Matter of Attitude

If selling is something we've done successfully since birth, why do 90 percent of all beginning salespeople eventually opt for another, less demanding career? It's a matter of attitude. Let me explain.

In my consulting work, sales managers often ask me why some of their salespeople hate to make sales calls so much. As I talk with their salespeople, I frequently find that they are suffering from what I call "reinforced fears of rejection."

When a prospect senses that a salesperson is selling more than he or she is helping the customer to make a logical buying decision, the prospect is likely to assume a defensive posture. Instead of being receptive to the positive features of the product, the prospect will focus on reasons he or she shouldn't buy. When a prospect assumes this attitude, the salesperson's job becomes extremely difficult—and it's usually the salesperson's fault.

Prospects don't want to be sold; they want to buy instead. Selling isn't a telling business; it's a motivational business. Consultive salespeople don't try to sell as much as they try to create an environment that will help prospects make positive buying decisions for their own reasons, not those of the salesperson. Aside from being an easier job altogether, it's also more lucrative.

There's an old saying among the world's successful consultive salespeople: *You can get whatever you want by helping enough people get what they want.* Consultive salespeople become successful because they help people get what they want. Mediocre salespeople drop out of the business because they don't help people get what they want. Instead, they try to manipulate their prospects into doing what the salespeople want, and there simply aren't enough prospects living today who are willing to be manipulated by mediocre salespeople.

Be a Friend

A person selling an idea to a friend will have an easier time than the person who is selling an idea to a stranger or, worse yet, an enemy.

People tend to resist any kind of change when they feel they're being sold. When prospects haven't accepted the salesperson as a trusted friend, they'll be more suspicious of the salesperson than they will be receptive to the possibility of buying what is being sold. On the other hand, if the prospect accepts the salesperson as a friend, then the prospect will be more open to the possibility of buying.

There's another old saying among salespeople that sums this up quite nicely: *People don't care how much you know, unless they know how much you care.* Consultive salespeople understand this fully.

So the formula for successful selling is being real or sincere. I'll bet that when you think about it, it's the way you've made every successful, mutually beneficial sale in your life, whether you were selling to an employer, a spouse, or a customer.

So how do you sell yourself? Do you go in and start talking about what a great person you are? Hardly! Remember what I said earlier. The best way to get prospects to like you is to get them to talk about themselves.

One of the quickest large sales I made, $5 million, was really closed because of using an expert communication skill—listening. I made my presentation but it didn't seem to have a tremendous impact on this particular wealthy prospect. He obviously had heard similar presentations many times before; there was nothing unique about mine. However, even wealthy people want to feel comfortable with the salesperson. Of course, it was one of my best presentations, so when I realized that he wasn't buying, I asked him about his success. For the next hour and a half, I listened to him talk about the obstacles he overcame to succeed. I finally did get the deal—the next day!

But let me back up and mention some other things about this particular sale. I did my homework. I learned that he had placed millions of dollars with a couple of other financial institutions in town, but he had never invested in ours. This was a repo investment, meaning that we had to place collateral in equal amounts to the investment. I learned from our investor that the maximum we had available for collateral was $5 million. I asked the corporate vice president to accompany me to the presentation in the event the prospect asked particular questions that I possibly couldn't answer. On the way over, I mentioned that I was going to ask for $5 million. The corporate vice president looked alarmed and said "You've got to be kidding! The most you should ask for might be $500,000." I realized then that he didn't have the confidence to secure that amount of money. So when I arrived at the prospect's office, I left the corporate vice president on the couch in the waiting room and went in and made the presentation alone. As I said, the presentation didn't seem to excite the prospect. I started to look around to see what made him tick. As I studied his office, I noticed that he had a substantial number of awards and plaques. Something that caught my eye specifically was a newspaper article about him that was framed in gold. The title said that he was "USED TO HANDLING BIG MONEY." I asked him, "What does it take for a person to have that big deal mentality?" And from there, for the next hour and a half, I listened intently as he shared with me the obstacles that he overcame to reach his success. He had quite an interesting story to tell and I did get the $5 million. When I walked out I winked at the corporate vice president. Today this customer, who taught me a valuable lesson about the big deal mentality, continues to be my friend. I learned that you have to have confidence in your abilities; you must do all of your homework; you must go the extra mile; and, in this case, you must be a friend. You have to be a nonconformist. A lot of other people simply would have made the presentation, shaken his hand, and followed up to find out that he invested his funds elsewhere. You have to be a friend to be a consultive salesperson. You have to listen intently but, as I said before, it's your confidence, imagination, and sensitivity to the client that will help you put together the big deals. The difference between a small sale and a large sale is simply your confidence to close it.

Seven Measures of an Image

Whether we're liked by others depends largely on our images. Certainly, we've all known people we came to like, even though at first we found their images offensive. But salespeople don't have the luxury of letting their prospects take months to get to know them. Therefore, they had better take great care in forming their professional images.

My corporate clients are very concerned about their companies' images and their executives' images in the marketplace because they know that customer acceptance or rejection quite often is based on those images.

Let's take a look at the seven points that make up an image.

1. *Appearance.*   First impressions are vitally important to a salesperson's success, and most of what forms one person's first impression of another hinges on appearance. The visual message we get from a person's appearance is lasting, especially if it's negative. A neat, well-groomed appearance won't put the sale in the bag; it's just the start of the sales process. However, a disheveled, sloppy appearance certainly can ruin your chances of making a sale. People will judge your company by your appearance. I know the old adage says that you can't judge books by their covers, but people do. Be neat, clean, and well-dressed. For business purposes, conservative clothing generally is best. A fashion-oriented client will forgive you for dressing conservatively much faster than a conservative client will forgive you for wearing the latest fads.

2. *Spoken words.*   Of course, what you say will be important. Choose your words carefully. Make them a part of the professional image you wish to project.

3. *Tone and emphasis.*   It's not what you say; it's how you say it. Don't we often judge people by their accents? My mother-in-law, a southern belle, says I am a Yankee. I don't start my sentences with an adjective or "Well, darlings"; I just jump right on in and start talking.

   As professional salespeople, we must be sensitive to other people's backgrounds and dialects and the com-

plexity of the English language. Let me share a secret
with you: the top 500 most commonly used words in
the English language have thousands of different
meanings. It is vitally important that we understand
what the customer is saying. Let's take the work "oh"
for example. A simple word, oh, has so many different
meanings: an oh that you use when you discover
something; an oh that you use when you agree with
something; an oh that you use when you disagree with
something; an oh that you use when you hit your
thumb with a hammer; an oh that you use when you
jump out of the shower onto wet tile; an oh that you
use when you see something quite unusual and
surprising.

In addition, dialects really do affect the way we
communicate. One afternoon, my grandmother was
driving south on I-71 toward her hometown of Derby
City. She's quite proud of Derby City and said to the
two little old ladies accompanying her, "Ladies, I wel-
come you to my hometown, Louavall." The lady sitting
in the front seat, a Yankee indeed, said, "Honey, it's
not Louavall, Its Louieville." My grandmother said,
"No, it's Louavall!" The Yankee lady said, "No,
Louieville!" Back and forth they went. Finally, just
when the little old lady in the back seat was getting
quite tired of this, they passed the green and white di-
rectory sign. She announced, "Ladies, I've got news for
you, the sign said Lewisville." This made my grandmother furious! Driving as fast as she could, she got
off the interstate at the first exit and came to a screech-
ing halt. She grabbed these two little old ladies and
dragged them into the establishment. She asked the
first man she saw, "Sir, tell me slowly and distinctly
where we are right now." He answered, slowly,
"BURGER KING!" So you can see how dialect and accents affect our perceptions of each other and our ability to communicate effectively.

4. *Actions.* What you do often says more than your words. Everything you do will be judged. Avoid nervous habits such as smoking, chewing gum, twisting a lock of hair, or biting nails. Act professionally to make a first-class first impression.

5. *Execution of actions.* Shaking a person's hand isn't enough. The manner in which you shake the hand tells much about you. A limp handshake indicates aloofness; a bone-crunching handshake indicates obnoxiousness. A firm grip indicates sincerity. No matter what you do, there is a right and a wrong way it can be done. Select the correct methods for fine first impressions.

6. *Environment.* Most people subscribe to the theories of "like attracts like" and "guilt by association." Of course, if you're meeting a prospect at his or her office, this won't be a problem (unless you bring a skid-row bum along for company). However, if you should ever have to suggest a meeting place for a prospect or customer, don't select the local beer joint or pool hall—even if you know the prospect frequents such establishments. After all, the prospect knows he or she is okay, but might not be too sure about you. Your environment is important. If you plan to take a prospect somewhere in your car, be absolutely certain that it is clean. If you offer a business card, make sure it's crisp and clean.

7. *Reputation.* This is one area where an ounce of prevention is truly worth a pound of cure. Keep your reputation clean, and you'll have no problem. If you don't, you'll likely have no career. Prospects are influenced by what others say about you. Establish a policy of dealing with people with flawless integrity. Keep your word with prospects. If you promise to send them information by a certain date, be sure you meet the deadline. No matter what you're selling, you have

plenty of competitors who will keep their promises.
Make sure your prospect doesn't seek out one of them
because he or she was dissatisfied with you.

Most people form opinions quite rapidly and usually will cling
to them even though they may have formed them with limited information. If they like what they see, they will continue to associate with you. If they don't, goodbye.

You are the company to your prospect. If you make a poor impression, the prospect might judge your company and its products
accordingly. Why take a chance?

The seven elements that form a first impression are under your
control. Be aware of what they are, use them to present an image
that is real, and you'll get their business.

Good Communication

A salesperson will be no more effective than his or her ability to
communicate, which means not only speaking effectively, but listening effectively as well. Communication is always a two-way exercise. It's important not only to be certain that you actually say
precisely what you mean, but to make sure you also understand
exactly what the prospect says. If there is any breakdown in communication, the sale might be jeopardized.

Most of the problems and arguments that occur can be attributed to poor communication. When people misunderstand
what is said or say things they don't mean, the result can be trouble, indeed.

Here are six common communication barriers that give us
problems.

1. *Incorrect thought.* The problem can begin at the
   source, with your idea. Are you correct in our thinking?
   Is the idea you have in mind valid and clearly defined?

2. *Chosen words.* If your words don't accurately convey
   your thoughts, you are communicating something dif-

ferent from what you're thinking. Just knowing what you mean to say doesn't necessarily mean that you've actually said it. Effective self-expression depends on using words that accurately reflect your thoughts. Be careful of trade jargon for example, "spots" can mean TV/radio ads, stains on your clothing, or even something a dog has.

3. *Emotional carryover.* Sometimes, communication can be hampered by body language, tone of voice, or emphasis. This is especially true if a previous statement has angered or upset you.

4. *Monotone.* A salesperson with a monotonous voice is about as effective as a barefoot tap dancer. Monotonous voices tend to lull listeners to sleep, which is precisely the opposite of what a salesperson must do to make a sale. Effective salespeople develop variety in their voices to keep their prospects alert and excited enough to make a buying decision. No one is going to want to buy anything if he or she can't keep from yawning.

5. *Insufficient volume and/or poor enunciation.* A salesperson who speaks too softly or enunciates poorly is simply wasting effort. Selling is effective communication, and if prospects can't hear or understand what is being said, it's virtually a cinch there won't be a sale.

6. *Preoccupied listener.* Sometimes, the listener is preoccupied and doesn't hear what is being said. Perhaps the listener is prejudiced against the speaker, angry, or simply resents what the speaker is saying. On the other hand, the listener might think that he or she already knows what the speaker is going to say and, thus, tunes out the message. In such a situation, the speaker must design the message to catch the listener's

attention. A mind is much like a telephone line. If it's occupied, no other message can get through.

Be aware of these communication barriers and deal with them effectively.

Feedback

Feedback is a response to information supplied by the speaker. At times, it might take the form of repeating what the speaker said to confirm that you have understood. This is a great tactic to use in avoiding misunderstandings. It's also a great way to show the prospect that you were paying attention to what he or she has said.

Feedback also can be a response in answer to a question or a statement. If the prospect offers no response to a statement, the salesperson must prompt a response with a question, such as "How do you feel about that?"

If you're in doubt about what is being said, don't hesitate to offer feedback. If you doubt that the prospect understands you, use a question to obtain feedback. Feedback is a great communication and sales tool.

When the Prospect Talks, Listen!

You can hear a dozen different people talk at the same time, but you can only listen to one at a time. Of course, most of your meetings will be one-on-one sessions with your prospects. Still, some salespeople tend to hear more than they listen.

One of the hardest skills to acquire is the skill to listen effectively. Here are some of my suggestions to help strengthen that skill.

1. *Listen for ideas.*   Facts are important, but the idea behind the fact is often more important. Don't put your mind on hold when a prospect starts spouting facts. By

listening carefully, you might detect an idea that can
lead to a sale.

2. *Look for the emotions behind the words.*   Often, what a
   prospect feels has more impact on the buying decision
   than what the prospect says. A person might be saying
   "no" when he or she actually wants to buy. The more
   sensitive you are to what a prospect is feeling, the better your chances of making the sale.

3. *Don't interrupt.*   One of the biggest mistakes
   salespeople make is interrupting their prospects. Perhaps the salespeople are eager to get on with the selling process, and, when the prospect pauses, they think
   they can supply the right words that the prospect
   seems to be seeking. This is not a good idea. First, the
   salesperson tends to tune out what the prospect says.
   Second, a prospect might be offended by being inter-
   rupted. And third, a prospect in the process of making
   a buying decision will be delayed by interruptions at
   best and discouraged at worst.

4. *Don't let delivery affect the content.*   In a sales situation, the message is more important than the manner
   in which it is delivered. Educational backgrounds and
   personalities can account for a variety of deliveries, but
   words are universal.

5. *Pay attention! Don't prejudge.*   Many people tune out
   speakers because they presume that they are boring,
   too trite, or otherwise have nothing significant to say.
   A salesperson so prejudiced against prospects' com-
   ments usually won't be in sales for long. Be interested
   in what your prospect says; there might be a sale in it
   for you. Doesn't that sound interesting to you?

If a salesperson's strength is in communication, then listening is vitally important. Listen effectively, and your effectiveness as a salesperson will increase.

Treat the Prospect Royally

Just as the best way to get prospects to like you is by getting them to talk about themselves, a good way to make an excellent first impression with prospects is by treating them like valued customers-to-be.

Here are three suggestions that have helped me to impress my prospects and close sales. Not a bad combination, is it?

1. *Do your homework.* Make it a point to find out all you can about your prospects—before your appointments with them. A lot of information might be obtained from the person recommending the prospect to you. If not, check out the prospect's chamber of commerce and local business or merchants' association for information.

2. *Don't shoot the breeze.* A sales appointment isn't a talk show. There's no need to entertain the prospect with a three-minute monologue. Start your sales interview by encouraging the prospect to talk about his or her needs and problems. You might hear valuable information that you can use to make a sale—and open the door to many future sales.

3. *Be a consultive salesperson.* If you want to increase your opportunity to make a sale as well as impress your prospect, gear your presentation to the needs of your prospect. You'll not only waste your breath by enumerating everything your product can do, but you'll bore your prospect as well.

Treat the prospect well, and continue to do so even after the sale. Successful long-term relationships with customers are the key to customer retention and repeat business. And they will open the door for you to their business associates and friends.

The first step of this mutually beneficial relationship is simply to sell yourself by getting the client to do the talking. Remember, it's the same thing you've done all your life in every relationship you've ever had. Don't sidestep this process in the important salesperson-prospect relationship, or there is likely to be no relationship at all. Sell sincerely.

Now that we've shown the importance of selling in our society, the components of a successful sale, and the importance of selling yourself first, let's take a look at the importance of the buyer. In the next section, we'll also discuss ways to find buyers and how to make sure they're treated royally.

Chapter in Review

1. Consultive salespeople don't try to sell as much as they try to create an environment that will help prospects make positive buying decisions for their own reasons, not those of the salesperson.

2. Consultive salespeople become successful because they help people get what they want.

3. People tend to resist any kind of change when they feel they're being sold. On the other hand, if the prospect accepts the salesperson as a friend, then the prospect will be more open to the possibility of buying.

4. The best way to get prospects to like you is to get them to talk about themselves.

5. Whether we're liked by others depends largely on our images. The seven points that make up an image are appearance, spoken words, tone and emphasis, actions, execution of actions, environment, and reputation.

6. A salesperson will be no more effective than his or her

ability to communicate, which means not only speaking effectively, but listening effectively as well.

7. Common communication barriers include incorrect thoughts, ill chosen words, emotional carryover, monotone, insufficient volume and/or poor enunciation, and preoccupation of the listener.

8. Feedback is an excellent tactic to use in avoiding misunderstandings. It's also a great way to show the prospect that you were paying attention to what he or she has said.

9. When a prospect talks, listen. Listen for ideas, look for the emotions behind the words, don't interrupt, don't let delivery affect the content, and pay attention and don't prejudge.

10. Treat the prospect/customer well, and you'll very likely be treated well by him or her.

Part II: Taking Care of Business

There are always two reasons people have for doing everything: the reason they state and the real reason.

J. P. Morgan

4

Discovering the Motivation Behind Buying

Where would a selling society be without buyers? Bankrupt, of course. The world would be full of frustrated salespeople.

As long as people have needs and the means to fulfill them, you might think that a selling society would be safe from insolvency.

However, in reality that is not true. People don't buy what they need. As strange as it seems, it's true. Statistics indicate that as many as 95 percent of all senior citizens retire from their jobs with a three-figure net worth—hardly enough to meet their needs for a month, let alone the rest of their lives. If those people had bought what they needed, they would have bought investments that would have provided them with income in their later years.

Why didn't they do that? The answer is simple. Instead of buying what they needed, they were too busy buying what they wanted.

Certainly, people need food, clothing, and shelter, and they buy them. But aren't their buying decisions based more on desire than on need? Ask yourself that question the next time you're ready to eat, the next time attractive apparel catches your eye, or the next time you're caught in the middle of a rainstorm without an umbrella. My mother used to send my father out for milk and bread. He would come home with bananas and cupcakes. Why? Because he wanted them! My husband does the same thing with gadgets, and I do the same thing with shoes.

People don't buy what they need. If they did, tobacco, alcohol, and illegal drug sales would cease, as well as purchases of numerous pleasure items of all price ranges. People would spend less for vacations, cars, and homes, and they would invest more in health care and long-term security.

No, people don't buy what they need. Instead, they buy what they want. It's important that you understand this before venturing out to sell in a selling society.

And, furthermore, I have found there are only four reasons why people want—and subsequently buy—anything. Let us examine them.

1. *Gain.*   People buy because they expect to gain something they consider worthwhile. They buy food to sustain them and for the pleasure of eating. They buy clothing to protect them from the elements and to project an image, and they buy homes for shelter and comfort. They also buy vehicles for transportation and numerous other items for pleasure and/or convenience. The big question is always, "What will I gain by giving up my money?"

2. *Pride.*   This is one of the strongest buying motivations. People who live in mansions don't necessarily enjoy better protection from the elements. Instead, they spend thousands of extra dollars to buy shelters that reflect their tastes and lifestyles. The same is true with cars. An economy car might be just as dependable as a high-priced luxury car, yet, many people opt for the latter because pride is their motivation for buying.

3. *Imitation.*   Most people buy for imitation. If keeping up with the latest clothing fashions appeals to you, imitation will be your motivation for buying clothes. Imitation is a strong reason for buying; if every other kid

on the block has a certain toy, it's a cinch your child will want one, too. This type of motivation carries over to adulthood, and many people go to great lengths to "keep up with the Joneses."

4. *Fear.* If people stopped buying out of fear, the nation's insurance industry would fold. In some parts of the country where winters are traditionally mild, grocery stores enjoy brisk sales when snow or ice is forecast. People buy more food than they'll need for fear they might be without. People buy expensive service contracts on merchandise because they fear that they'll be hit with more expensive repair bills if they don't.

Your success as a salesperson will be enhanced by knowing these four reasons for buying, recognizing which one will motivate your prospect, and gearing your presentation accordingly.

You Must Be Sold Before You Can Want

If you recognized a desire for a product, what would you do? Go out and buy it? In a retail situation, yes. But you'd better believe that the product was sold to you somehow. If millions of dollars invested in advertising the product didn't sell you, you probably got a good report on it from a friend or associate. In any event, you must be sold before you can want. Most people will never express a need for anything they don't want.

In nonretail situations, advertising might be limited or nonexistent. Therefore, prospects may not know they want the product, simply because they aren't aware that it exists or of how it can benefit them. In short, they haven't been sold on the product.

Inexperienced salespeople quite often ignore their prospects' strongest motivations for buying. Because they don't understand and often won't discuss the prospect's personal situation, the salesperson has a natural tendency to try to sell one product or service that would solve all of the prospect's problems. Of course, the prospect isn't plagued with most of the cited problems, if he couldn't care less about the solutions. The result? No sale.

Old-Time Selling

Long ago, before consumers became so sophisticated and competition became as intense as it is today, salespeople would spend a token amount of time, if any at all, discussing the prospect's situation and personal desires. They would spend far more time making elaborate presentations designed to show off their vast product knowledge and even more time using manipulative tactics to close the sale.

Successful salespeople today know that these tactics no longer work, simply because today's alert consumers won't put up with them. The world is full of competition, both in terms of products and salespeople. If either one offends the customer, he or she may simply try another.

In a creative sales presentation, prospects may not understand fully how acquiring your product could benefit them. Even if they do, they may not have enough information about your product or service to justify purchasing it at the present time—the best time to make a sale.

Therefore, your first effort must be directed toward helping a prospect become aware of his or her desire for your product, whether it's based on gain, pride, fear, or imitation. Only then will he or she be receptive to a sales presentation that is geared to personal desire.

Of course, if the person who recommended the prospect can give you some insight in this area, that's great. But most often, you'll be faced with the responsibility of finding out for yourself the prospect's motivation to buy.

Consultive Salespeople Consult

Unless you have a crystal ball, the only way you'll discover the prospect's motivation to buy is by asking. Your questions should be designed to yield information that will help you determine how your product can best suit the prospect. This is a part of consultive selling that separates pros from amateurs. Consultive salespeople help their prospects select the right products or services to accommodate their particular desires.

Later, I'll devote an entire chapter to the probing process, which, if done correctly, is clearly the most time consuming aspect of the sales process. But for now, understand the importance of getting information from the customer. A canned presentation, or a sales pitch designed to appeal to the masses, is built on the assumption that the salesperson and prospect are standard models and quite representative of all buyers. In a retail situation, this might be true; witness the number of television commercials, magazine ads, and billboards that offer the same messages to the masses. After all, laundry detergent, fast foods, and toilet bowl cleaners have rather limited uses, regardless of the prospect.

But in a nonretail situation, products often have various features and applications, and a particular aspect that would be of benefit to one prospect might be undesirable to another. If this weren't the case, a good canned presentation would not be offensive to anyone, and the most successful salespeople would be those with the best memories. As a result, selling wouldn't be one of the most exciting and demanding careers available, as it is today and as it will likely remain in the future.

Why People Don't Buy

One reason I find selling so exciting and demanding is because prospects don't always buy. Part of the thrill of selling is that success isn't guaranteed. Therefore, whenever you go into a sales interview, your adrenaline will be flowing and your palms may even be a little sweaty. It's a little like the feeling you get when you watch a tightrope walker or a trapeze artist perform at the circus without a net. Even though the aerial artist might be expertly trained, there's no guarantee that he or she won't fall. The same is true for the salesperson. Although the salesperson may be expertly trained, there's no guarantee of a sale.

When people don't buy, there is a reason. And the quote from J. P. Morgan at the beginning of this chapter applies here as well: There are always two reasons people have for doing everything: the reason they state and the real reason.

Prospects may state a million different reasons for not buying. But I find that there are only four real reasons for *not* buying:

1. *No confidence.*   The customer isn't convinced that the product or service will be satisfactory, that the salesperson is trustworthy, or that the company is reliable and dependable. Thus, one of your biggest challenges is always to build trust—for you, your company, and your product or service.

2. *No need.*   Remember, people don't need anything they don't want. If the prospect doesn't feel a desire for the product, there will be no sale for you. The smart salesperson always tries to uncover a prospect's deepest desires and then builds his or her presentation around those desires.

3. *No money.*   Lots of us want things we can't afford. That's one of the things that keeps us motivated to succeed in a selling society. However, that doesn't help the salesperson who is trying to make a sale today. Naturally, if the customer can't afford the product, there will be no sale. That's why it is most important to qualify prospects as early as possible during the sales interview. It's the only way to make sure you spend most of your time with prospects who have the resources and authority to buy whatever you are selling.

4. *No urgency.*   A prospect might be confident that your product or service will meet a definite need (desire) he or she feels, and might have the money to buy, yet delay because he or she feels no sense of urgency to

act. To be successful in this business, you have to be
able to give your prospects many strong reasons to act
at the time of your presentation. The best way to overcome the no urgency problem is to build so much
value that the prospect feels he or she simply must
have what you are selling, and the sooner the better.

In an upcoming chapter on handling objections, I'll show you
more specifically how to deal with each of these reasons for not
buying. For now, note them to understand better why people in a
selling society choose not to buy. When you understand these reasons, you'll be better able to gear your presentations so they will
satisfy these potential objections before they surface.

The Big Marketing Picture

Marketing is the set of actions by individuals and/or organizations
that enable, facilitate, and encourage an exchange to the mutual
satisfaction of both parties. Yet, we just covered several reasons
prospects often resist such transactions.

Depending on the situation, these four reasons—no confidence,
no need, no money, and no urgency—might or might not be linked
to factors beyond your control. Let's explore them.

1. *Economic conditions.*   If consumers truly aren't willing
   to part with their money for any reason, there is little a
   salesperson can do. Salespeople can do their best to
   change a prospect's attitude, but even successful
   salespeople can't do that all the time. At best, they can
   always try again later and constantly search for prospects who will buy.

2. *Nature.*   If, for example, you run a ski shop in the
   mountains, but the weather has been balmy, business
   is going to be bad, and there's little you can do about
   it. The same is true for golfing during rainy weather.

3. *Government.* When the government imposes tariffs on certain imported goods, your sales expertise might be challenged if you're in the business of selling these goods. You'll have to convince your prospect that your product is worth the increase in price. Government regulations also can be a hassle. Potential owners of firearms, airplanes, and two-way radios have to be convinced that ownership is worth the hassle and expense involved with compliance.

4. *Competitors.* No matter what advancements your competition makes, the only thing you can do is your best. And you should be doing that anyway, regardless of the competition.

5. *Society.* The actions and reactions of society are powerful. Hula hoops and pet rocks were once the rage, and sales were brisk indeed. How would you like to be selling them now? If you're in the business of selling fads, it might be a good idea to keep your résumé current.

6. *Technology.* It was a sad day indeed for the slide rule salesperson when he or she learned about the invention of pocket calculators. Electric typewriters, once considered the greatest invention since sliced bread, are now on their way to obsolescence, thanks to modern-day computers. And this can happen to any of us. As a successful salesperson selling word processors, I took a beating when computers arrived on the market; they offered much more for much less money. When technology makes an advance, the only thing an affected person can do is react.

It pays to keep abreast of developments in these uncontrollable areas and to prepare for them, if possible. However, since they are uncontrollable, I've found it more profitable to spend more time trying to control the four factors that are within the control of the typical salesperson or organization.

1. *Value.*   If records show that price is a common objection to sales, it is usually because salespeople are not building enough value to make prospects willing to part with their money.

2. *Place.*   Selling requires attention from the prospect. If the sales setting isn't conducive to concentration, the effort is likely to be a waste of time. Successful salespeople avoid selling in office lobbies or in crowded, noisy restaurants. They insist on a setting that is more conducive to selling and buying.

3. *Product.*   Successful salespeople don't complain because their products aren't selling. They know how to make prospects recognize their need for them. When successful salespeople can't sell products because of declining desire (such as the hula hoop or slide rule), they find other products to sell.

4. *Promotion.*   A product without sufficient promotion probably won't stay in production for long. While promotion of products and services is primarily a concern of company executives, salespeople can do much to promote themselves and their products. By using sales literature and product information sheets fully, they can keep their names and products before customers and prospects constantly. Also, sending testimonial letters from satisfied customers will do much to attract the interest of skeptical prospects.

The job of marketing consists of managing or controlling the emphasis on the controllable four (sometimes called the marketing mix) to capture your share of the market. Up-to-date knowledge as to what and how the business environment is changing is essential to good marketing management.

To identify clearly the salesperson's role in the marketing picture, the element of promotion must be broken down into its four elements.

A. *Advertising*.   The salesperson must know and actively work to support the company's advertising programs.

B. *Selling*.   The salesperson must secure the most advantageous position and use sales promotional material as much as possible.

C. *Sales promotion*.   The salesperson must sell the full line of products, with particular emphasis on items targeted by advertising and sales promotion.

D. *Publicity*.   The salesperson must work to build public acceptance of his products.

It's a salesperson's responsibility to help keep selling his or her company's products and services. And sales will keep right on occurring in our society, as long as there are enough interested buyers.

But where do you find them? The next chapter will cover this in detail.

Chapter in Review

1. People don't buy what they need. Instead, they buy what they want.

2. There are only four reasons why people want—and subsequently buy—anything. People buy to gain, for pride, to imitate, and out of fear.

3. Prospects may not know they want the product, simply because they aren't aware it exists or of how it can benefit them. In short, they haven't been sold on the product.

4. Successful salespeople today know that manipulative

sales tactics no longer work, simply because today's alert consumers won't put up with them.

5. A salesperson's first effort must be directed toward helping a prospect become aware of his or her desire for a product or service.

6. Consultive salespeople help their prospects select the right products or services to accommodate their particular desires by consulting with them. A canned sales pitch won't work anymore.

7. The four reasons people don't buy are no money, no need (or desire), no confidence, and no urgency. These reasons might or might not be linked to factors beyond your control, such as economic conditions, nature, government, competitors, society, or technology.

8. A salesperson or sales organization can control four factors related to the sales process: value, place of sale, product, and promotion. These four factors are known as the marketing mix.

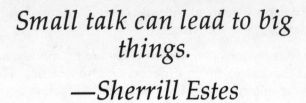

Small talk can lead to big things.

—Sherrill Estes

5

Secrets to Networking
for Success

As a consultive salesperson, you will retain customers through the development of long-term relationships. In relationship selling, I believe not only should you have good relationships with your customers but also with your co-workers. In my office equipment selling days, many relationships were strained between the service and sales departments. I believed that since the service department was out there servicing my customers every day, it was vitally important that I maintained a good relationship with them. One afternoon, the service department turned in a very large lead. One of my customer's systems was old and breaking down and my service person suggested that I visit them. I did and sold them more than $100,000 worth of new equipment. In talking with other sales professionals, I've heard them complain that their service departments didn't turn in leads promptly or develop a good relationship with their customers. Perhaps that's because the salesperson took the service department for granted. I've learned along the way to build a win-win relationship with all of the people who deal with my customers. My service person was extremely pleased when I gave him over $1,000 for helping me out. After that, he consistently looked for opportunities for me.

However, you must continue to add to your base of customers because of attrition that is out of your control.

Customers have a way of disappearing over a period of time. Some of them change jobs, leave town, are bought out, go bankrupt, become disillusioned with your product or service (sorry, but it can happen to anyone), get lured away by the competition (yes, this happens, too), retire, or even die.

Some studies indicate that a salesperson's list of customers will decrease by 20 percent each year through attrition. This means that if you have 300 clients on January 1 and add no new ones during the course of the year, you will only have 240 clients when the next New Year's Day rolls around. For various reasons, sixty of them will no longer be doing business with you.

Additional customers can be added through networking.

Secret to Networking

Suppose I told you a secret, and you immediately told two people. Tomorrow, those two people each would tell two people, and the next day, those four people each would tell two people, and so on. At the end of a month, do you know how many people would know my secret? Would you believe more than five million people?

Now, suppose I give you the name of a prospect, and that prospect gives you the names of two more prospects. Upon contacting them the next day, each of them gives you the names of two prospects, who each give you the names of two prospects, and so on. At the end of the month, you would have more than five million prospects.

Of course, both of these examples are unrealistic if taken literally. I mean, anyone who can come up with five million prospects per month—or any month, for that matter—can write his or her own book on sales, and I'll be quite happy to read it. However, the point of this illustration is to show the power of networking. Even if you get a prospect who doesn't buy, chances are good that he or she could recommend to you a prospect who might purchase, who could recommend another prospect who might purchase, and so on.

Just one lead can open the door to a long list of clients, especially if the prospect turns out to be a satisfied customer. And, of course, that's the constant goal of consultive salespeople.

If your customer is truly satisfied with your product or service and the way he or she was treated, that customer could spread good reports about you to many others.

And how do you find the names of these people? Simply ask a satisfied customer. Of course, he or she probably won't be able to recommend hundreds of people to you, but even one could be enough to get you started. After all, each prospect you receive also has a pool of hundreds of friends and associates, and so does each of them.

The bottom line? Clearly the best source for prospects is a satisfied customer. So now you understand that treating the customer fairly is important not only to protect the account, but also to help insure your future success. It's a safe bet that you'll get absolutely no prospect recommendations from someone who feels that you have treated him or her unfairly.

Ask Properly

Of course, the way you ask is important. After all, it might be hard to think of all the people you know who might be able to use a particular product without a little coaxing. The mind is very complex, and it's responsible for processing a great deal of information on any given day.

So when you ask for prospects, don't say, "You don't know of any people who could use my product, do you?" Such a question almost sets up the asker for a negative answer. In fact, it wouldn't be much better to ask, "Do you know of anyone who could benefit from our product?" Again, it's hard to pinpoint one or two likely prospects from a field of hundreds of people or more.

Be specific. A good networking question is, "Do you know anyone among your close friends or in your office, bowling league, church, social or civic clubs, or neighborhood who might be able to use our products?" Such a question will get the prospect thinking specifically of the people with whom he or she comes into contact.

As a result, the person will be better able to make recommendations.

Lead Sources

Aside from satisfied customers, here are some sources I've used to generate leads:

1. *Customers in general.* Customers who buy for the first time may not know whether they are satisfied until the product arrives. Don't let that stop you from asking for prospects. If you've built enough trust to close a sale, you can almost count on getting one or two good leads. And don't forget to keep asking your regular customers for additional prospects.

2. *Prospects who don't buy.* A prospect who doesn't buy truly might not have a desire for your product. That doesn't mean that he or she has anything against you. You might find that prospects who don't buy can have a positive effect on your income by recommending to you prospects who will buy.

3. *Inactive customers.* A great source for prospects is your list of clients whose accounts have become inactive for whatever reason. Find reasons for revisiting them, such as introducing a new product, service, idea, or application. Review your old call reports and orders. If they have become inactive because they were dissatisfied with your service, see if you can do something to make amends. If they're particularly angry, let them vent their frustrations and then try to help them solve their problems. In most cases, you're likely to find that you'll get a warmer reception from old customers than from new prospects.

4. *Friends.* Don't hesitate to ask your friends for prospect recommendations. If they are any kind of friends

at all, they won't mind being asked, and they'll be
most eager to help you. After all, a prospect recommendation costs absolutely nothing, but it can go a
long way toward boosting your income.

5. *Publications.*   No matter what you sell, there is almost certainly some publication geared toward your
particular industry, be it a trade journal, newsletter,
or magazine. Check those out for potential prospects,
along with the business section in your sales
territory's daily newspaper.

6. *New acquaintances.*   Certainly, it would be in poor
taste to start selling at a party or other social function.
However, there is nothing wrong with introducing
yourself and, during the course of conversation, letting
the person know about your business.

7. *Other salespeople.*   A terrific source for new prospects
might include other salespeople, provided they are not
in competition with you. For example, if you sell pho-
tocopiers, there would be nothing wrong with asking
an office furniture salesperson for prospects. After all,
you might be in a position to help the salesperson as
much as he or she could help you.

When you think about it, do you know anyone who wouldn't be
a good source for prospects? As long as they are breathing, they're
worth the question.

Of course, if they give you a lead, be sure to thank them. If the
prospect turns out to be profitable, you might even give them a reward, whether it be cash, a discount, dinner, flowers, or whatever
might be appreciated. But never fail to thank people for recommendations. Otherwise, they may feel that you are taking them for
granted and may take their business—and prospect
recommendations—elsewhere. You certainly wouldn't want to
dry up a good prospecting source, would you?

One caution in asking for referrals: never mistreat a prospect whose name was given to you by a friend or customer. Nothing closes off your flow of referral leads quite as effectively as does a reputation for offending the people whose names you have been given.

Direct Mail

As I have mentioned, using a direct mail campaign helped me sell millions and millions of dollars in the financial industry. I call it the "mail-call-close" approach. Because I sold so many different kinds of investments, I needed to automate my accounts. Thanks to the computer, I could send out 500 "automated but personalized" letters a week. I would spend every morning on the phone qualifying and preselling my prospects. Eventually I only closed the big deals personally and used office staff for the smaller investors. And as a consultive salesperson, I would send a car out to pick up elderly customers. Many times, they brought along another wealthy prospect.

One way to make more sales is through a disciplined and consistent direct mail program. If you conduct such a program within your territory, you can achieve the following benefits:
- You will get your name in front of prospects on a regular basis.
- You will create an awareness of your company and its products or services.
- You will generate a percentage of inquiries from qualified prospects.
- You will pave the way for a telephone approach later.

Let's take a look at how I contacted and sold so many people by using an effective direct mail program.

1. *Do it regularly.* There is no point to sending out mail to more people than you can telephone later. Of course, if your letters are effective they may call you— but don't count on it. The direct mail is just a warm-up for your call. Remember, the key is to send out only as

many letters as you can possibly follow up on. Nearly every person I sold received a letter first.

2. *Target your program.*   Devise your mailing list so that it consists of people most likely to use your services. The better the prospect, the more likely the sale. I don't believe in sending out mail that doesn't look personalized or is not targeted.

3. *Follow up with a telephone call.*   Many successful sales representatives wait three days after dispatching the mail and then follow up by telephoning the prospect. Most prospects won't take the time to make a return call, but many will agree to an appointment if you call.

4. *Personalize your mail.*   Writing a personal note on your brochure or letter generates a better response. Use your computer to generate a variety of letters for each product or service. I used to tell my secretary that these 100 people should receive letter A, these 200 receive letter B, and so forth. Automate your mail and personalize it.

5. *Include your name, business address, and telephone number.*   Don't make it hard for the prospect to contact you. If possible, include a response card to make it even easier for the interested prospect to answer.

6. *Always use commemorative stamps.*   Direct mail experts say that this tactic improves the percentage of returns by a considerable margin. Why? It stands out and looks more important than the regular bulk-rate mail most of us receive.

7. *Prepare mail during nonselling hours.*   Don't miss out on sales because you're too busy trying to reach new prospects. Prepare your mail during off hours as an investment in your career, or hire a secretary.

Follow these tips for a successful direct mail program. I understand, of course, that this might be a massive undertaking for some salespeople, who might be overworked or who have a penchant for leisure time. If you don't intend to follow through, then a direct mail program will not only be wasteful, but expensive as well. If you favor sending out only a few pieces of mail each week because you don't have time to follow through on more, then send the mail out on a Tuesday and make your telephone calls on Friday. But if you, too, want to become a super salesperson, then start it now.

The Pre-Approach

Once you get a good lead, the pre-approach step to the sale begins. The pre-approach step is when a salesperson compiles information that he or she can use in the initial meeting with the prospect. This step can save you considerable time. The alternative is to discover this information when talking to the prospect for the first time. The more you know about your prospect, the more quickly you'll discover which products can best help him or her. Why waste time?

As I mentioned earlier, a good information source is the person who recommended the prospect. In addition to that (or in lieu of that, if you came up with the prospect on your own), you might consult the local chamber of commerce or merchants' association.

Precall Planning

Before I telephone a prospect to make an appointment, I want to accomplish five objectives. These objectives will help you maximize your effectiveness at making appointments.

1. *Qualify the prospect.* This is most important. If the prospect isn't able to buy the product, there's no point in wasting time trying to sell it. Qualifying the prospect means making sure the person has the resources,

authority, and a strong reason to buy at the time of your call.

2. *Prepare your initial benefit statement.* This is the statement that is designed to heighten the prospect's interest, so that he or she will be more likely to make an appointment. I'll go into detail on this in the sales section. (Ladies, remember the line, "Haven't I seen you someplace before?")

3. *Prepare fact-finding questions.* Any information you haven't discovered yet might be determined over the telephone. Make a list of questions designed to elicit what you need to know.

4. *Prepare your sales message.* Design a general message that will stress the benefits of your product, relying heavily on sales vocabulary. (We'll cover that in the sales section.)

5. *Prepare your request for an appointment.* Don't ask if the prospect would like to make an appointment. Instead, offer a forced choice question, such as, "Could we meet at 3 p.m. Thursday, or would Friday be better?" It makes it harder (not impossible, though) for a prospect to refuse an appointment when a question doesn't allow for that option.

Make sure that your approach is mapped out carefully so that you will sound businesslike over the telephone or in person.

Schedule for Calling

People operate on different schedules. Naturally, as a salesperson, you'll want to contact your prospects during the time that is most suitable for them—that is, when they might be most likely to react favorably to your request for an appointment.

One of the best sources I used was a study conducted among

various types of professions that reveals the best time to call particular prospects. When setting up appointments, refer to this table to improve your appointment—and, I hope your sales—batting average.

- Advertising Account Executives and Media Representatives—after 3 p.m.
- Architects—late afternoon
- Artists—2:30-3:30 p.m.
- Assistant Personnel Directors—early afternoon
- Auditors and Certified Public Accountants—between the 12th and 20th of each month
- Bankers—before 10 a.m.
- Brokers—before the New York Stock Exchange opens
- Chemists—late afternoon
- Claims Adjusters—between 9 and 11 a.m.
- Clergymen—midweek (they're doing homework on Saturdays and selling on Sundays!)
- Commission Merchants—after 2:30 p.m.
- Contractors—late afternoon or 7:30 a.m.
- Convalescent Home Operators and Employees— 1-3 p.m.
- Dairy Executives—late afternoon
- Dentists—call on days off before 10 a.m.
- Department Store Personnel—8:30-9:30 a.m.
- Dietitians (hospital)—1-3:30 p.m.
- Doctors—days off or 11 a.m. to 1:30 p.m.
- Executives—between 10:30 a.m. and 3 p.m.
- Grocery Store Employees—Tuesday or Wednesday from 1 to 3 p.m.
- Jewelers—mid-morning
- Lawyers—before 10 a.m. or after 4 p.m.
- Movers—from the fourth to the eighth of the month or between the 17th and 22nd of the month (avoid Mondays)
- Newspaper People—early afternoon for both morning and evening papers.
- Night-Shift Superintendent—4 p.m.

- Personnel Directors—early to mid-morning
- Production People—10:30 a.m.
- Publishers and Printers—after 3 p.m.
- Purchasing Agents—early morning, except Mondays and Fridays
- Real Estate Executives—mid-morning of mid-week
- Retail Store Owners—30 minutes before opening (urban); around noon (suburban)
- Surgeons—mid-afternoon
- Teachers—after 3 p.m.
- Theater Owners and Managers—before 2 p.m.
- Traffic Departments—1-3 p.m.
- Wholesalers—before 10 a.m. on Saturdays

You'll fare much better with your prospects by making an appointment that won't interfere with their prime times. After all, they're busy making a living, too.

And when you find prospects, you'll want to stay on good terms with them. That's how you build repeat business, and that's the topic of the next chapter.

Chapter in Review

1. Successful salespeople know how to network, which means finding new customers to replace old ones.

2. Just one lead can open the door to a long list of clients, especially if the prospect turns out to be a satisfied customer.

3. Most people have a sphere of friends and associates that totals hundreds of people. This could help or hurt a salesperson's prospecting efforts, depending on how he or she treated the customer.

4. Ask for prospects. The best source is a satisfied customer. Other sources include customers in general, prospects who don't buy, inactive customers, friends,

publications, new acquaintances, and other (noncompeting) salespeople.

5. Using direct mail is another way to find prospects. If you begin the effort, follow through and be consistent.

6. When you get a lead, find out as much as possible about the prospect before meeting with him or her. This information can save you time and help you make a sale.

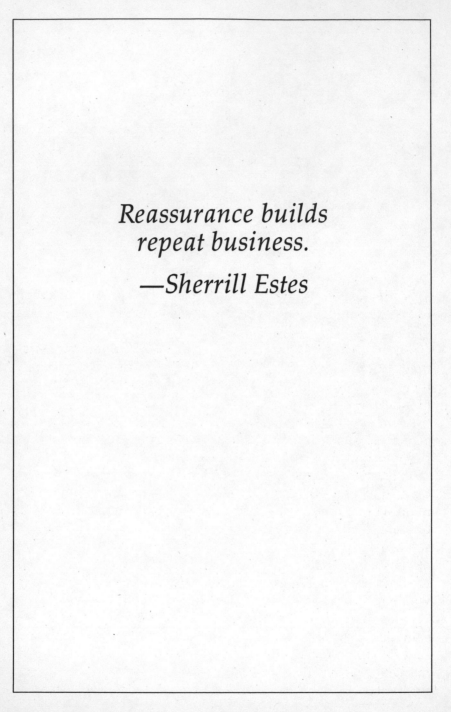

*Reassurance builds
repeat business.*

—Sherrill Estes

6

Building Repeat Business Easily

No matter what you sell, you sell more than a product or a service. Successful salespeople also sell good will. They know that making a single sale is only the first goal they must accomplish, because that one sale is only a drop in the bucket compared to what they could get from a succession of sales to a steady customer. And there's only one way to keep a steady customer: by making sure that he or she is satisfied.

Another situation that happened to me early on in my selling career reinforces the point of the long-term relationships and repeat business. I sold dictaphones in the legal market. My closing ratio on trials (that is letting the person try out the systems) was close to 95 percent. Naturally, I was most discouraged one afternoon when I had to remove a particular system from a lawyer's office. I reached in my briefcase and realized that I didn't have a screwdriver to unhook the system. I went next door to one of my old customer's to borrow one. As I visited with the receptionist, my customer walked out of his door and said, "Sherrill, it's really wonderful to see you. I was just thinking about calling you. Do you have a moment?" I answered, "Sure I do. I need to take care of something, but I'll be back in a few minutes." When I returned he said he was interested in a word processor (we had just started marketing word processors). We had had one salesperson on staff for the last six months trying without any luck to sell our word processors, and she had just resigned because she was burned out and frustrated. Our word processors were new in the marketplace and we had tremendous competition. I knew that getting one word processor in the market would lead to many sales, so it was very important to me to sell this particular word processor. My customer purchased a $26,000 dollar system based again on our long-term successful relationship. I had serviced his accounts with other systems and he believed in my ability as his consultive salesperson. His confidence in me was quite evident the day I went to pick up the check, accompanied by a new sales manager. As my co-worker reached to pick up the check and signed agreement, my customer promptly put it in my hands. As we left the customer's office, the new sales manager smiled and said, "You have a tremendous relationship with your customers. I see that they trust you." Of course that was true; having had him as a customer for many years, I had serviced his needs time and time again. This was just a larger deal that evolved through helping him build his business by saving him money and time through the use of innovative systems he had purchased along the way. Thanks to his testimonial as a satisfied customer, we were able to sell many more word processors.

If a customer is unhappy with any aspect of a particular transaction, you will lose more than just a customer. You very well might lose many other customers and potential customers as well.

To add credence to this point, consider a study conducted by Technical Assistance Research Programs, Inc., a Washington, D.C., company that conducted a business study on customer satisfaction—

- Officials of the average business never hear from 96 percent of their unhappy customers. In fact, for each complaint received, the study indicates that there are twenty-six other customers with problems—six of which are considered serious.
- Dissatisfied customers who don't complain are less likely to do business again with the company than those who register complaints.

- The average customer with a complaint tells nine or ten people about it. Thirteen percent of dissatisfied customers tell more than twenty people.

Sound scary? It should. The situation could be compared to termites at work on a house. The homeowner might not be aware of the problem until it becomes extremely expensive to solve.

But on the brighter side:

- Between 54 percent and 70 percent of complaining customers will do business again with the offending company if their complaints are resolved. If the company makes amends swiftly, the percentage increases to 95 percent.
- Customers whose complaints are resolved tell an average of five people.

More and more of my corporate clients are requesting customer service programs for their sales staff. The real sales pro knows the value and importance of building good will. I have found that satisfied customers will give me leads and help me to penetrate my market.

Why Customers Disappear

Another survey shows why people stop doing business with companies. Of all customers who cease relationships with a business, only 1 percent can be attributed to death. Some 3 percent of the customers move to another area, and 5 percent take their business to a competitor who is a personal friend. Complaints account for 9 percent of lost customers, and dissatisfaction with the product or service accounts for 14 percent. Finally, 68 percent of the customers who never come back are offended by the attitude or actions of the business representative(s).

Consultive salespeople aren't interest in one-shot sales. They are interested in building relationships that will survive in the future. They know that is definitely the easiest—if not the only—way to remain successful in the sales profession.

Successful salespeople are always aware of the law of reciprocity, which states that for every thing you give, you will get something of equal or greater value. They know that any giving that's required of them to build good will is very likely to be given back to them in the form of future business. They know that by placing the highest importance on customer satisfaction, they can build a relationship that will survive most inconveniences to the customer, such as a price increase or a temporary service slowdown.

The customer who is treated fairly and well by the salesperson will make such concessions more willingly than the customer who feels the salesperson is only out to make a buck—any way he or she can.

Everything for a Purpose

Amateur salespeople often say that their purpose is to make money. That's the main reason they're amateurs. With dollar signs in their eyes and mental images of signed contracts in their heads, they focus more attention on techniques for closing sales than on customer satisfaction. Of course, such techniques lead to aggression when prospects hesitate to buy, and the pressure eventually erodes the salesperson's effectiveness. As a result, many of them eventually seek other careers.

Consultive salespeople know better. I'm not going to tell you that they don't enjoy money, because they do. They know sales is a profession that can provide them with as much income as they are willing to earn.

But earn is the operative word. Consultive salespeople know that the only way they can earn income over the long term is by helping—not tricking or intimidating—the customer to make a buying decision. That's the consultive salesperson's purpose—to help people buy and to make customers as happy with their products or services as salespeople are to receive their income.

Amateurs build self-esteem through attaining sales quotas, money, plaques, trophies, and other symbols of success. They regard these symbols as their purpose. Yet, many amateurs don't get a lot of these symbols. However, to the consultive salesperson, such symbols are only goals that can be achieved through dedication to their purpose. As a result, they can set long-term goals, be more productive, and get more rewards than the salesperson who only gets excited about money.

Building good will not only will help assure your future success with clients, but it will help determine your present success as well. By being most concerned with satisfying your client, you will shine by comparison, and your customer will view you as standing head and shoulders above the amateurs.

Win-Win

The first rule of building good will is to engineer win-win relationships between you and your client. Of course, when you get the sale, you win. But if your client is unhappy with the transaction, you have won at his or her expense. That is known as a win-lose transaction, with your client on the short end (although you will be the big loser in the end when your client starts dealing with another salesperson).

Only through consultive selling can you create a win-win situation. It is only by determining your clients' wants and expectations through meaningful dialogue that you can be sure your products will solve their problems and, thus, create a win-win situation.

Think about personal relationships for a moment. Win-win relationships are the only ones in which people prosper. When a friendship or marriage ceases to be a win-win relationship, it usually ends. When a job is no longer a win-win relationship, the employee either quits or is discharged, depending on who was on the losing end. When a professional, such as a physician or attorney, offers unsatisfactory performance, the client often files suit, because the client feels (either justifiably or unjustifiably) that the transaction was a win-lose relationship.

As a professional salesperson, you simply cannot afford win-lose relationships. Although you may get fat in the short run, you'll starve in the long haul.

Build good will by building win-win relationships.

And if the Customer Loses . . .

Try as you might, there will be times when the customer becomes dissatisfied with your service through no fault of your own. Mistakes can and will occur from time to time.

But the real mistake in such a situation is not correcting the original mistake. Remember the survey cited earlier. Ninety-five percent of complaining customers will resume business with a company if they feel that their complaints are resolved quickly and satisfactorily. Those are not bad odds.

Of course, you want to avoid mistakes. But when they do happen, don't make the mistake of ignoring them. When a client calls with a problem, solve it quickly and cheerfully. If the problem cannot be solved instantly, at least let the customer know you will get on it immediately.

Don't Let Clients Hurt Themselves

I heard a story once about a new salesperson who paid his first visit to a client. As the story goes, the salesperson had barely gotten through the doorway before the client chased him out of the store. The salesperson did some investigating and found out why: his predecessor had talked the client into buying more inventory than he would be able to sell in three years. The sight of the dead stock and the sting of a tight cash flow were enough to make the client a sworn enemy of every salesperson who worked for that company.

The story ends happily, however, because the new salesperson built good will. He found a merchant who was willing to buy the surplus products at cost from the overloaded client. As a result, the client became one of the 95 percent of dissatisfied customers who resume business relations after the company makes amends.

The moral of the story? Never intentionally oversell to anyone—even if the client is inclined to overbuy. Amateur salespeople would take the money and run, but sooner or later, they have to come back, and it's not likely to be a pleasant situation when they do.

Even if the clients willingly placed the order, you can bet that they will hold you responsible if you encouraged them to overbuy. When you believe clients are overbuying, let them know that you believe they can get by with a smaller order. The future sales you can make from such a strategy will make the one you willingly forfeited seem like small potatoes in comparison.

Offer to Help

When someone does you a favor, you are grateful. Furthermore, if you get the opportunity, you probably will be only too happy to help the person should he or she ever need a favor in return.

Such is the way of the power of selling, and that goes double for professional salespeople. With your vast product knowledge, you probably are in a position to make all kinds of suggestions to help your prospects and customers solve problems, save time and money, increase production, and sell more products in general.

It won't cost you a thing to part with your suggestions; however, such suggestions might benefit your prospects and customers immensely. Furthermore, when it comes time to buy again, they will think of you as an expert in your field (which you are), more than just a salesperson, and you just might become their exclusive supplier.

Be willing to help. It's good for your reputation—and your income.

Go the Extra Mile

One way to avoid dissatisfaction with your product is by taking every opportunity to make sure the customer doesn't get the opportunity to be dissatisfied.

I have always believed that it is a good idea to be on hand when a product is delivered. If you're present, you can make sure it's in excellent condition and installed properly. Also, you can make sure that the owner knows how to operate it. If you're not present, there is always the chance that the product could be installed incorrectly or even be damaged. Even if the customer is at fault, you'll get the blame for not showing him or her the proper procedure for operation.

Go the extra mile for the client. Your willingness to serve your clients will show that you value their business and will prompt them to deal with you the next time they need your products or services. Make delivery not only the last step of the sale, but the first step of the next sale.

In all my experience, I have found that nothing frustrates a customer more than trying to figure out how a product works. If customers just wanted to buy boxes and assemble the products themselves, they would buy from retail establishments and put you out of business.

Stay in Touch Regularly

Amateur salespeople spend so much time calling on accounts they want to win that they neglect and lose accounts they already have. Obviously, this isn't the path to success.

Don't take your good customers' business for granted. There are plenty of competitors today who won't take your customers for granted if they get the chance to move in on them—which they will, if you're guilty of customer neglect.

To make sure you spend enough time with your clients, it might be a good idea to rate them in terms of their orders and potential orders. Let me share with you a secret to putting your customers into perspective:

- "A" customers are those for whom your company is the exclusive supplier. If you've ever seen a salesperson cry, it's probably because he or she lost one of these.
- "B" customers are good, solid customers who buy frequently and have the potential to become "A" customers.
- "C" customers buy occasionally. As time goes on, they may increase their orders, provided you serve them

well. They also have good potential to be upgraded to
B or A customers.
- "D" customers are marginal customers. Their pur-
chases are few and far between.

Of course, you don't want to lose *any* of your customers. But
there is only so much time in a week, and if you have to ignore or
neglect any customers, it's obvious that it should be those with the
lowest rating. However, you can keep in touch with lower rated
customers by telephone, while saving your time for personal visits
to your better customers.

It is possible to overservice an account, as I pointed out earlier. I
wouldn't recommend asking a customer how often you should
call. If you act on the customer's recommendation and the customer should be in need between calls, you might lose a sale—if
not an account—to a competitor.

Use your own judgment when determining how often to visit.
Thanks to Mr. Bell, you can always alternate personal visits with
telephone calls to check on clients.

Learn Your Lessons

Sure, you'll make mistakes from time to time. But, as I said earlier,
don't make the second mistake of not correcting your first mistake.
Furthermore, don't make the third mistake of not learning from
your first. All mistakes offer lessons, and successful salespeople
learn from them. Amateurs try to forget them.

They say that life's best lessons are the hardest to learn. However, you can learn some good, and even profitable lessons by
learning from your competitors' mistakes. Whenever you land an
account that was lost through a competitor's mistake, find out
what it was and learn from it.

Mistakes are good teachers, especially when your competitors
make them. By the same token, however, you can also learn from
your competitors' successes. When you can't get an account because a customer is dealing exclusively with a competitor, you can
make your effort worthwhile by asking why the customer favors

the other company. Listen to the answer, and take notes if necessary. Salespeople don't get exclusive customers without good
reason.

Long-term successful relationships happen because you make
them happen. Satisfied customers are the key to positioning you as
a pro, giving you leads, and creating lasting success. I positioned
this chapter where it is—immediately preceding the sales
section—to illustrate the importance of building lasting success.
Before you turn the page to learn about actual sales techniques, I
want you to understand that your purpose is building a list of satisfied customers. Never forget this if you want to be successful.

And now that you understand this, it's time to sell!

Chapter in Review

1. If good will doesn't exist, customers not only will seek
    out competitors, but also will be likely to encourage
    their friends to do the same. On the other hand, if a
    customer feels wronged or taken advantage of, restor-
    ing good will can be healing.

2. Of all customers who quit doing business with a com-
    pany, 68 percent of them were offended by the atti-
    tude or actions of the business representative(s).

3. Consultive salespeople aren't interested in one-shot
    sales. They are interested in building relationships that
    will survive into the future.

4. The first rule of building good will is to engineer win-
    win relationships between you and your client.

5. Always look out for the client's best interests—before
    and after the sale. Don't let the customer overbuy, and
    if a problem develops with the sale, resolve it quickly.

6. Offer suggestions having to do with your field to your
    prospects and customers. It won't cost you anything,

but it can provide you with the opportunity to make many future sales.

7. Go the extra mile for the customer. When equipment is delivered, be on hand to check it, if possible, and, if necessary, supervise its installment.

8. Always visit the customer soon after the sale. It will show that you're truly interested in the customer, and it will give you the opportunity to reassure him or her that buying the product or service was a wise decision.

9. Always stay in touch with your customers. Rate them in terms of profitability and potential profitability, and pay the most attention to your best customers.

10. Learn lessons from mistakes—both yours and those of your competitors. Also, learn from your competitors' successes.

Part III:
Making the Sale

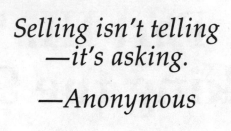

*Selling isn't telling
—it's asking.*

—Anonymous

7

Getting Them Interested in You

As I've learned, people don't buy what they need; they buy what they want. Contrary to popular belief, salespeople cannot make prospects want something they have no desire to own. However, if there's even a chance that a prospect might feel a spark of interest in buying your product or service, a skillful salesperson knows how to fan that spark into the flame of desire.

It isn't done through sorcery; it's done by asking questions. Selling isn't a telling business; it's an asking business. To create an atmosphere conducive to motivating their prospects to buy, salespeople must ask questions to find out about their prospects' needs and desires. And in so doing, successful salespeople can make prospects aware of their desire for the product or service.

Once this is done, the salesperson's job is halfway finished. As noted salesperson Frank Bettger once said, "Show people what they want, and they'll move heaven and earth to get it."

But make no mistake: this is no easy task. A successful salesperson must be equal parts psychologist, investigative reporter, physician, and attorney. The common link among these professions is that people practicing them must ask questions to prompt their clients to talk about areas of concern, overall objectives, specific needs, problems, and readiness to act. Salespeople must have this information from prospects to communicate meaningfully how their products and services can satisfy their desires.

There are several other reasons a salesperson should be skilled at asking questions. A salesperson must ask questions:
- To determine if the prospect is able to buy. (As pointed out in the prospecting chapter, this often is done on the telephone when making an appointment.)
- To get feedback from the prospect.
- To handle objections.
- To determine the prospect's buying attitude and when to close the sale.
- To ask for the order.

All questions solicit information. Of course, they should be asked in a courteous and nonthreatening manner, but the way they can be structured varies a great deal and will have a significant effect on the results achieved.

The Power of Questions

Questions are a powerful tool for salespeople. They accomplish many objectives.

A. *Questions obtain information.*   With the right questions, you can qualify your prospects with regard to their likelihood, ability, and authority to buy. You also can determine who is involved in the buying decision, the time frame for the decision, and any special requirements or restrictions.

Properly phrased, open-ended questions also will draw out the customers' goals as they relate to your product or service; identify specific desires; uncover problems that you can solve; and bring out the underlying reasons for prospects' questions, stalls, and objections.

B. *Questions keep the prospect actively involved.*   They can establish rapport and stimulate dialogue. Through thoughtful questioning, you can get a feeling for the customer's personal style, so that you can interact with him or her accordingly. Questions will make customers feel significant in the selling process and will ensure that they pay attention and follow your thought process. Salespeople who tell instead of sell often find their prospects' minds tending to wander. Prospects who are lectured lose interest, while prospects allowed to participate in the sales process tend to stay interested.

C. *Questions allow the salesperson to control the selling situation.*   They'll help you determine which product or service to present (if you offer more than one), determine which benefit(s) to stress, confirm your understanding of the prospects' statements through feedback, and evaluate the prospects' thinking about acceptance or rejection of products or services. Actually, finding out this information is the key to consultive selling. Finally, questions provide salespeople with the means to use the customer's reasons to lead to the close.

Successful salespeople know how to ask questions skillfully. By understanding the power of questions, you will have taken the first step toward mastering the art of selling.

Set the Stage

Before you get the chance to ask questions, you'll have to earn the prospect's attention by arousing his or her curiosity at the beginning of the interview. Sales experts say that, of all sales lost, 97 percent of them are lost in the first ten to twenty seconds of the interview because the salesperson never obtained the prospect's attention and interest.

Remember, prospects don't buy because your product is good; they buy because your product is good for them. Prospects always want to know how they'll benefit from a product. They want to be sure that the benefits they receive will outweigh the price they must pay.

Therefore, your knowledge of the prospect and product must be combined to form an initial benefit statement designed to capture the prospect's attention and raise his or her curiosity.

The value of an effective initial benefit statement would be difficult to overstate. It earns a good audience and establishes the conditions for your face-to-face information gathering. (Used over the telephone, it can help you get an appointment with the prospect.)

Of course, the initial benefit statement should focus on how the product or service will help the particular prospect. The product, for example, should be able to save the prospect time and/or money or help the prospect earn more money through its use.

You can tell how effective your initial benefit statement is by the reaction or feedback it produces. There are four possibilities.

1. *A question.* If I say that a product will save time or money, the prospect might respond by asking how the product works or what is the product. This shows that the prospect is at least curious. (When trying to stage appointments with prospects over the telephone, don't answer this question. The answer is your ace in the hole to get an appointment. Simply state that there are many reasons for these benefits, and the prospect's business is too important to deal with them over the telephone. Then ask for the appointment again.)

2. *A challenge.* The prospect may resist your benefit statement by challenging it. For example, "It won't work here," or "We tried something like it last year, and it didn't work." Actually, a challenge is almost always a good sign. Think about it. How did the prospect reach the opinion that the product or service wouldn't work? The prospect tried it, because—at least at one time—he or she was interested in it. And this interest can be rekindled if you can show the prospect how your product or service will work.

3. *A pause.*   A pause indicates the prospect is likely to be thinking positively, such as, "I wonder if it would work." This is the kind of listener you want.

4. *A rejection.*   The "I'm not interested" response tells you that your initial benefit statement missed the target. Always have one in reserve, just in case the one you've chosen doesn't connect with the prospect's highest interest at the moment.

An initial benefit statement is important, even when calling on inactive accounts. The prospect's interest might be superficial, but it often can be heightened by a good initial benefit statement.

Plan your initial benefit statement in advance. This is the beginning of your presentation. Don't rely on luck. As someone once said, "Your first ten words when meeting another are more important than your next 10,000. In fact, if the first ten words aren't the right ones, you either won't have a chance to use the next 10,000 or you will waste them." Talk in terms of the prospect's interest, and you'll earn the right to a good interview.

The Four Types of Questions

There are four types of questions a salesperson can use to interview a prospect.

1. *General questions.*   These are questions that are designed to get people to open up and discuss their overall goals, circumstances, and problems.

2. *Specific questions.*   These questions obtain concrete, specific information about situations, attitudes, and needs.

3. *Probing questions.*   These questions are designed to uncover deep problems, wants, and feelings. They also can be used to pinpoint critical issues, some of which the customer may not even be aware of.

4. *Leading questions.*   These questions will focus customers' perceptions of wants, help the customer articulate
   them, and prompt the customer to make choices.
   Leading questions (in the form of feedback) also can
   verify your understanding of the situation and obtain
   customer agreement.

Questions are powerful, if you know how to ask the right ones at
the right time. Understand how the four types of questions can be
used for maximum effectiveness during an interview.

Questions: Open-Ended and Closed-Ended

Although there are four different types of questions, any given
question is either open-ended or closed-ended, depending on the
way you phrase it.

Open-ended questions can help you pinpoint the prospect's desires, needs, and interests. These are questions that can't be answered with a yes or a no. The prospect must elaborate.

Let me cite a verse from Rudyard Kipling that's quite appropriate
for describing open-ended questions.

> I keep six honest serving men
> (They taught me all I knew);
> Their names are What and Why and When
> And How and Where and Who.

When you begin a question with the words "who," "what,"
"when," "where," "why," or "how," you'll get an answer about people, action, time, place, reason, or method, respectively.

Closed-ended questions, on the other hand, are questions that
must be answered with a yes or no. These questions begin with
words such as "is," "are," "do," "has," "can," "will," and "shall," and
they are good for confirming specific information and getting
commitments from prospects.

Structure Questions Correctly

During the fact-finding portion of your interview, it's important to structure your questions correctly. If you don't, you might wind up with only a portion of the information you need. Here are four tips on how to phrase your questions for maximum effectiveness.

1. *Avoid closed-ended questions early in the interview.* Even if you know the answer to a question, it might be better to ask the prospect an open-ended question at the beginning. Closed-ended questions tend to limit customer participation to a yes or no. Too many of them might make the prospect feel that he or she is being interrogated.

   When a closed-ended question comes to mind, you can make it an open-ended question by adding one of the six open-ended question beginners—who, what, when, where, why, and how. For example, take the closed-ended question, "Have you heard about our product?" By adding one word, the question becomes open-ended—"What have you heard about our product?" This way, you get two answers in one. You not only confirm that the prospect has heard about your product, but you also find out exactly what he or she has heard.

   Don't ask questions like, "May I help you?" "Are you unhappy with your supplier?" or "Are you planning to make a change?" Instead, ask "How may I help you?" "Why are you unhappy with your supplier?" "When are you going to make a change?"

2. *Use caution in asking leading questions.* A question like, "Why do you think this equipment is good?" might set you up for an incomplete answer. The prospect might think there are some negatives to the equipment. However, since the question only calls for the good points, the prospect may not tell you about the bad points. In such a case, use an open-ended

question instead, such as "What do you think of the equipment?" Don't presume anything from the prospect. Be objective in your questioning. (Of course, toward the end of the interview—after you've obtained your facts—it's fine to use leading questions to help you close the sale.)

3. *Don't let your reasoning show.* If the prospect can see the reasoning behind your questions, he or she might feel manipulated. For example, the question "Why do you like this copying machine?" permits the prospect to give the answer he or she thinks the salesperson wants to hear. On the other hand, it gives the prospect the chance to mislead the salesperson deliberately. A better question would be, "How would you rate this copying machine?"

4. *Keep your questions short.* Long questions can confuse prospects. Consider this one: "In order for me to get a complete understanding of your problem, could you describe, in detail, the various reasons that prompted you to decide on the course of action you took to overcome your difficulties?" Wouldn't it be better to ask, "How did you solve your problem?"

Word your fact-finding questions so that they will encourage elaboration and won't seem manipulative. If you make them objective and easy to answer, you can discover some very valuable facts that can help you close a sale.

Exercise Caution

Sometimes, questions can cause you problems, depending on the circumstances or the way you ask them. Let's examine a few ways that certain questions can cause problems.

1. *Some questions can offend the prospect.* A prospect can feel manipulated—and rightfully so—if an encyclope-

dia salesperson asks, "Are you interested in obtaining a good education for your children?" Furthermore, it's poor salesmanship, because an offended prospect can stop the interview cold by saying, "No, I want them to remain idiots for the rest of their lives!"

2. *Some questions can frighten the prospect.* A salesperson who asks a woman what time her husband will be home might be mistaken for a burglar or a rapist. Think carefully about the questions you ask.

3. *Questions can get talkative prospects off on tangents.* Sure, you might get information, but you also may have to listen to a lot of stuff you don't want or need to hear. I try to use the topic of the tangent as a means of getting the prospect back in the sales process. For example, if a question about the prospect's business leads to an elaborate discussion on how the business has grown, I would ask, "Would you be interested in learning about a system that would help you control your business?"

4. *Questions can reinforce negative feelings.* You've always heard it said that one should never discuss politics and religion. Other potentially volatile issues include race, personal problem areas, and, sometimes, the economy. If your prospect starts thinking and talking on a negative vein, you might have a difficult time making the sale. To keep your prospect positive, choose your questions carefully, avoid volatile topics, word your questions so that they will yield positive answers, and focus on solutions more than problems.

Questions are powerful. But, like anything with power, they can also be dangerous. Avoid the negative use of questions by learning how to use them correctly. Here are some pointers.

a. *Move from broad to narrow questions.* Ask open-ended questions first to prompt the prospect to elaborate on his or her situation and desires. When a clear desire begins to surface, ask closed-ended questions to pin down the specifics.

b. *Ask the question, then listen for the answer.* Although this suggestion might seem elementary, you'd be surprised at the number of salespeople who ask questions, then frequently interrupt the prospect while he or she is trying to answer. Some salespeople even jump in to answer their own questions. You can't learn anything from prospects if you're not willing to listen.

c. *Keep questions simple and deal with a single issue at a time.* Don't play "stump the prospect." It's a game you can only lose. Make sure the prospect is able to answer your questions by keeping them easy to understand.

d. *Be sensitive when asking seemingly insensitive questions.* A prospect might be threatened to hear the question, "How much can you afford to spend for a widget?" Whether the answer is $10 or $10 million, the prospect is likely to feel intimidated, because the question is asked in a condescending manner. The same question can be asked in a way that won't threaten the prospect. "How much do you plan to invest in a widget?" is a question that shouldn't offend anyone.

e. *Make it easy for prospects to voice concerns.* Studies show that prospects will give affirmative answers more readily to questions that reflect their concerns than they will express them voluntarily. If you sense that your prospect is resisting the sales process for a particular reason, you can work toward solving the problem by helping the prospect verbalize his or her concerns through closed-ended questions.

The more easily the prospect can answer your questions, the easier it will be for you to close the sale. Follow these guidelines when preparing your questions to enhance your chances of making the sale.

So, now that you've obtained your facts from the prospect, the next chapter will show you how to make a powerful presentation.

Chapter in Review

1. Successful salespeople know how to discover a prospect's desire for a product or service by asking questions.

2. Questions elicit information, keep the prospect involved, and allow the salesperson to control the selling situation.

3. An initial benefit statement arouses the prospect's curiosity, earns the salesperson a good audience, and establishes the conditions for a face-to-face information session.

4. The effectiveness of an initial benefit statement can draw one of four responses: a question, a challenge, a pause, or a rejection. Its effectiveness can be judged by the response.

5. There are four types of questions: general, specific, probing, and leading. Any given question also may be open-ended or closed-ended depending on how it is asked.

6. When gathering information, avoid closed-ended and leading questions. Conceal your reasoning from the prospect, and keep your questions simple.

7. Be careful how you ask questions. Under certain circumstances, they can cause problems. Know how to use them correctly.

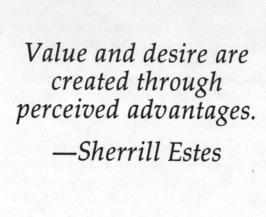

*Value and desire are
created through
perceived advantages.*

—Sherrill Estes

8

Making the Presentation Powerful

People buy because of what they perceive the product or service will do for them. For example, none of us would spend big bucks for a fine suit, only to display it on a hanger. Instead, we buy a suit because we believe that we will look good in it.

In short, sales are made only after a customer realizes what the product or service will accomplish and decides that he or she is willing to pay the price for those benefits.

Sometimes this can happen without the aid of a salesperson, depending on the interest of the customer. Most of the time, however, it takes a salesperson to help the customer realize his or her desire to own the product.

Of course, I've pointed out already that a benefit to one person may be insignificant to another, and that successful salespeople gear their presentations to appeal to individual customers. In this chapter, you will discover you can do that.

Features, Advantages, and Benefits

Once you've gained your prospect's attention with your initial benefit statement, the burden of proof is on you. You must satisfy your prospect that your initial benefit statement is an accurate assessment of the benefits to be offered by the product or service and not a trumped-up claim.

The best way to start this is by learning to view your product or service in three parts: features, advantages, and benefits.

A feature is a physical characteristic of the product or service. It could be a handle, a storage compartment, a hard disk, a speaker, certain hardware, a tilt steering wheel, a provision in an insurance policy, and so on. Generally speaking, any portion of the product or service that can be expressed as a noun is regarded as a feature of the product.

An advantage is a performance characteristic that results from the feature. For example, an advantage of a handle on an item might be ease in transporting. A storage compartment's advantage would be more storage space. A hard disk offers the advantage of faster computer functioning, a policy provision provides payment under certain conditions, and a speaker's advantage includes sound reproduction. As a rule, an advantage is most often expressed as an adverb, verb, or adjective.

All customers will agree on features and advantages (provided they can be proven). However, the resulting benefit may not be perceived as a benefit, depending on the individual customer's tastes and desires.

For example, the feature of a five-speed transmission with overdrive might offer the advantage of decreased fuel consumption. However, the benefit of saving money won't appeal to the person who prefers the ease of driving that an automatic transmission offers. Conversely, the feature of an automatic transmission offers the advantage of not having to bother with changing gears. But the benefit of simpler operation wouldn't appeal to a person who prefers the action of changing gears, better control over the vehicle, and saving money on fuel.

A benefit is a personalized value. Remember, when a customer wants to know "what's in it for me," he or she really is asking, "What's the benefit?" When customers ask for benefits, they don't want to know each and every one. Instead, they just want to know the benefits that pertain to their desires—the only real benefits that exist for them. And you should know their desires from the interview.

Let me give you a formula sentence that will help you remember the difference among features, advantages, and benefits: "Because of *the feature*, the product will offer *the advantage*, which means *the benefit*." Let's say that we're talking about a dishwasher with an energy-saving control. The sentence would read, "Because of *the energy-saving control*, the dishwasher will offer *decreased energy consumption*, which means *you'll save money in energy costs*.

The better you can articulate features, advantages, and benefits, the better you will be able to communicate to your prospects exactly how your product or service can serve them and, thus, help them recognize their desire to own it. When that happens, the sale is virtually in the bag.

Some Prospects May Be Skeptical

Depending on your product or service and the nature of your prospect, you may have to prove your stated claims before the prospect will even entertain any notion of buying. When this is the case, you'll have to offer evidence.

Evidence is anything the salesperson does or any information he or she might offer that would prove the stated benefit. Of course, evidence in the sales business is like benefits; what constitutes proof to one customer very well might not convince another customer at all. Therefore, the salesperson must select the proof that will be accepted by a particular prospect.

Here are ten common proofs. Odds are good that at least one of these proofs will satisfy even the toughest prospect. I carried a sample of these in a "sight seller" or portfolio, and I recommend them to you. I still use many of these today in regular mailings to prospects. Here they are.

1. *List of previous customers.*   Some customers can be influenced to buy upon seeing a long list of other customers who have bought similar products or services. Build your own list by asking your customers if they would allow you to add their names to your list. This is

especially helpful if you do not work for an established
or major company.

2. *Testimonial letters.*   Nothing carries influence like a
satisfied customer. Ask your satisfied customers if they
will write such letters, spelling out the benefits they've
received, to help persuade new buyers. Many will
oblige. Even those who don't care to write such a letter
might agree to sign a testimonial letter that you have
written, provided that the letter is composed tastefully
and doesn't read like a thirty-second radio commercial.

3. *Third-person stories.*   Save any and all newspaper and
magazine articles by experts about your product or
service. People tend to place a lot more faith in what
they read than what they hear. An expert can make
the difference. My husband and I were on the patio
listening to the radio. I said, "Wow! It's really hot. It
feels about 95 degrees." He gave no response. Shortly,
an announcer on the radio said the temperature was
95 degrees. My husband said, "Can you believe it's
that hot out here?" I said, "Yes, that's what I just said."
He said, "But you're not on the radio!"

4. *Charts and graphs.*   Prospects love visual proof, even if
it's nothing more than a jagged line that signifies
growth or reliability.

5. *Photographs.*   Photographs are good forms of proof,
depending on the product. After all, one picture is
worth a thousand words.

6. *Guarantees.*   A guarantee from a reputable company
can settle potential doubts and fears before they
arise. Warranties can help you build credibility for
your claims.

7. *Exhibits.*   This is a good form of proof, particularly if
the product or service is put to a public test. Exhibits

usually include facts and statistics about the product or service that might ease a buyer's skepticism.

8. *Sales literature.* This is just another form of advertising. Customers feel secure with products that manufacturers spend advertising dollars on. Also, brochures, specification sheets, and other sales aids usually contain significant information to answer most buyers' questions.

9. *Samples.* Possibly the best proof is a sample, because it allows the customer to be the ultimate judge, a judge the customer can truly trust.

10. *Demonstrations.* During my years of selling office equipment, demos were a daily occurrence. Even today in my speaking business, I invite meeting planners into many of my sessions. A demonstration is good proof.

Remember, what will convince one person might not faze another. Therefore, it will be to your advantage to build your collection of evidence so that you can prove your claims even to hard-to-convince prospects.

Confirm It

Once you've convinced your prospect that your claims are valid, then take advantage of the situation by confirming it. Simply restate the benefit in question form that is designed to get a yes answer.

For example, suppose you've proven that your service will save the prospect time and money. After that point is proven, you might say to the prospect, "Don't you agree that this service will save you time and money?" (By the way, lawyers use these questions all the time. In court, they're called leading questions.) Of course, if the prospect says no, you haven't proven your point.

In addition to being leading questions designed to elicit yes answers, confirming questions also are good ways to determine whether good communication has occurred. When your prospects agree with your statements, you will know that you have communicated with them effectively. One word of caution: this technique is used to help the customer make a decision and receive feedback on his decision and should not be used to trick your customer. As a consultive salesperson you are there to build trust!

Sell, Don't Buy Back

Stating features, advantages, and benefits is usually when most salespeople get into trouble. During this phase, which is sometimes called the conviction step, it's easy for the salesperson to get carried away describing the features, advantages, and benefits that he or she likes, but in which the prospect has little, if any, interest. To put it another way, a salesperson can spend five minutes selling a product and twenty-five minutes buying it back.

A good salesperson will know a great deal about the product or service that he or she may not mention to any given prospect, simply because he or she knows the prospect isn't interested. For example, a particular stereo system might be good for people all ages. However, a salesperson who stresses to an elderly couple its ability to rattle windows at high volumes most likely will lose the sale.

Of course, it often is tempting to impress your prospects with your vast product knowledge, but it's seldom productive to smother them with a multitude of facts and figures in which they have no interest. Gear your presentation to suit their desires, and keep in mind the importance of features, advantages, and benefits.

Positive and Negative Words

When you were a child, you probably learned quickly that there were some words (most of them containing four letters) you were not allowed to use, or you would get your mouth washed out with soap. As salespeople, we know that there are other words we shouldn't use, lest we run the risk of losing the sale.

Here is a list of such negative words. If any tend to pop up in your selling vocabulary, it might be a good idea to find a more positive substitute for them.

abandoned	fear	precipitate
abuse	flagrant	prejudiced
affected	flat	premature
alibi	flimsy	pretentious
allege	fraud	retrench
apology	gloss over	rude
bankrupt	gratuitous	ruin
beware	hardship	shirk
biased	harp upon	shrink
blame	hazy	sketchy
calamity	ignorant	slack
careless	illiterate	smattering
cheap	imitation	split hairs
collapse	immature	squander
collusion	implicate	stagnant
commonplace	impossible	standstill
complaint	improvident	straggling
crisis	insolvent	stunted
crooked	in vain	superficial
cut-and-dried	liable	tamper
deadlock	long-winded	tardy
decline	meager	timid
desert	mediocre	tolerable
disaster	misfortune	unfair
discredit	muddle	unfortunate
dispute	neglect	unsuccessful
evict	negligence	untimely
exaggerate	obstinate	verbiage
extravagant	odds and ends	waste
fail	opinionated	weak
failure	oversight	worry
fault	plausible	wrong

Avoid these negative words. They are sales killers. If you need positive words to substitute for them, perhaps you'll find them in the next list.

ability	effective	life
abundant	efficient	loyalty
achieve	energy	majority
active	enhance	merit
admirable	enthusiasm	meritorious
advance	equality	notable
advantage	excellence	opportunity
ambition	exceptional	perfection
appreciate	exclusive	permanent
approval	expedite	perseverance
aspire	faith	pleasant
attainment	fidelity	please
authoritative	fitting	popularity
benefit	genuine	practical
capable	good	praiseworthy
cheer	grateful	prestige
comfort	guarantee	proficient
commendable	handsome	progress
commendation	harmonious	prominent
comprehensive	helpful	punctual
concentration	honesty	reasonable
confidence	honor	recognition
conscientious	humor	recommend
cooperation	imagination	reliable
courage	improvement	reputable
courtesy	industry	responsible
definite	ingenuity	satisfactory
dependable	initiative	service
deserving	integrity	simplicity
desirable	intelligence	sincerity
determine	judgment	stability
distinction	justice	substantial
diversity	kind	success
ease	lasting	superior
economy	liberal	supremacy

through	unstinted	vivid
thought	useful	wisdom
thoughtful	utility	you
thrift	vigor	yours
truth	vital	

Use positive words to help put buyers in a positive mood *and* a buying mood.

Here are some additional words that I use that generate positive results: *"discover," "easy," "free," "health," "love," "new," "no-risk," "now," "productive," "results," "safety,"* and *"savings."*

Avoid Trite Sales Phrases

Trite sales phrases lack the power you need to close sales. Such phrases are used by stereotypical used-car and seedy door-to-door salespeople. (Perhaps one reason we tend to think of those salespeople in that way might be the fact that they use trite phrases so often.)

These phrases automatically turn off most, if not all, prospects, mainly because they are poor persuasion tactics. Let's take a look at some of them and discover why they produce the opposite of the desired effect.

1. *You can't run your business without it.*   Not true. The business has survived so far, or the salesperson wouldn't be talking to the prospect about the product. Furthermore, the prospect very well might continue to operate the business without the product, just to prove a point.

2. *These things are as hot as two-dollar pistols.*   Not only is this a hackneyed phrase, but it compares the product with a cheap and dangerous item known as a Saturday night special. Definitely not good salesmanship.

3. *The demand for these is money in the bank.*   If so, why is the salesperson selling instead of living it up on the French Riviera?

4. *These products are selling like they're going out of style.*   Does that mean they are about to become obsolete? This phrase actually says nothing.

There are many other overused, trite phrases, but you get the picture, I'm sure. It's a good idea to avoid them. It's also a good idea to avoid "trust me" selling. The prospect has absolutely no reason to trust you until you prove that you can be trusted. And the only way you will gain such trust is by honorable, truthful selling.

When selling, stick to features, advantages, and benefits. That's a tested and proven tactic for success.

Of course, regardless of what claims you make and how much evidence you present, customers don't always buy right away. Some don't buy at all, and others won't buy without offering a variety of stalls and objections, which you must overcome if you are to make the sale.

The next chapter explores in detail the differences between stalls and objections and how you can handle both successfully.

Chapter in Review

1. A feature is a part of the product or service that offers an advantage, which results in a benefit to the user. Prospects are not interested in all benefits—only in those that will do them good.

2. With skeptical prospects, salespeople will have to prove their claims. Evidence must be geared to the individual prospect and might include a list of previous customers, testimonial letters, third-person stories, charts and graphs, photographs, guarantees, exhibits, brochures, samples, and demonstrations.

3. After proving a benefit, confirm it by phrasing the benefit in the form of a question that calls for an

agreement from the prospect. It helps put the prospect in a buying frame of mind, and it's also a good way to determine that good communication has occurred.

4. Stick only to benefits that interest the prospect. Those are the only benefits that exist for him or her.

5. Don't overload prospects with facts. Get them interested in the product, and let them ask questions. Then start selling!

6. Learn the positive selling words and use them. Learn the negative selling words and avoid them. Avoid trite sales phrases too.

Accept the challenges, so that you may feel the exhilaration of victory.

—General George S. Patton

9

Expect Challenges and Turn Them into Sales

General Patton was one of the greatest salespeople who ever lived. He sold the concept of combat in such a way that soldiers were happy to buy it. And make no mistake, that took serious selling.

Of course, Patton probably had his own way of dealing with people who stalled or offered objections. And while those methods worked in the army, they probably wouldn't be effective (or even legal) for salespeople who get stalls and objections from their customers.

There's quite a difference between the two situations. Patton's soldiers didn't have a choice. If they refused to fight, they could be court-martialed and punished for willful disobedience of orders. Customers, on the other hand, can refuse to buy for any reason they choose, and they can walk out of the store—or usher you out of their offices—without even saying good-bye.

Successful salespeople don't have that problem, because they know how to handle stalls and objections. It isn't easy, but this is part of what makes selling as tough a profession as it is rewarding.

Yes, stalls and objections are indeed challenges. Many sales are lost because salespeople don't know how to handle them effectively. But if you can "accept the challenges," as General Patton said, you can also "feel the exhilaration of victory."

Objections are facts of life in the sales profession. Successful salespeople expect and even prepare for them before their interviews with prospects.

Of course, I can't and won't list in this book every objection I've ever heard. You wouldn't have the strength to pick up the book if I did. However, I will tell you that if you keep the customer's best interests as your first priority, you'll find yourself being able to handle almost any objection that comes your way.

Defining Challenges

What's the difference between a stall and an objection? A stall is the prospect's stated reason for not buying, while an objection is the real reason. Remember what J. P. Morgan said: "There are always two reasons people have for doing everything: the reason they state and the real reason."

Of course, there is always the possibility that the prospect's stated reason for not buying *is* the real reason. If that is the case, then you can treat it as an objection; I'll show you how to do that later.

The Anatomy of a Stall

Sometimes you can get stalls early in the sales process—especially if you're selling or trying to make an appointment over the telephone. Such stalls generally come from people whose interest you didn't gain with your initial benefit statement. If you are to make the appointment and/or the sale, you'll have to cut through these stalls.

Let's examine several of the stalls that tend to pop up early in the sales process, along with the responses I've used over the years that have worked time and time again for me.

1. *I'm not interested.* "I wouldn't expect you to be interested until I've had an opportunity to explain how this product can save you time and money."

2. *I buy from a friend.* "That's fine, some of my custom-

ers buy from several companies. Suppose I show you a product that will increase your profits and give you even greater value?"

3. *I'm satisfied with our present supplier.* "Great, can you tell me what you like about your present supplier? If you could change anything about your present supplier, what would that be?"

4. *I'm already using a competitive product.* "That's all the more reason you should want to see everything that's available, Ms. Prospect. That way, you can be assured of getting the product that is best suited to your particular needs. Can you tell me your reasons for selecting that product?"

5. *I can't buy everything.* "No one can buy everything, Mr. Prospect. But people should buy those products that serve them best and deliver the most profit or satisfaction. I'm offering exactly that type of product..."

6. *Business is bad.* "I'm sorry to hear that, Ms. Prospect. However, this product can help you increase your business."

The best way to avoid such early stalls is to develop an interesting initial benefit statement. Of course, no one bats a thousand, and when initial benefit statements fail, successful salespeople know how to handle the stalls that are likely to result by offering another benefit statement. Be ready to use several when making a call.

Objections

Many salespeople get defensive when they hear objections. Actually, objections are prospects' positive contributions to the sales process. First, objections keep prospects talking, and second, objections keep attention focused on the product or service.

It's only natural for prospects to question price, delivery dates, product credibility, and other product-related factors. Sometimes, prospects offer objections based on insufficient or incorrect information. Occasionally, you'll find that a prospect has no use—or at least isn't aware of one—for the product or service.

These are valid reasons for not purchasing. And, if you give up when objections are raised, you'll never close a sale. But successful salespeople know how to overcome objections by giving additional information, correcting incorrect information, or by helping the prospects realize a desire for their products. When a prospect offers a negative comment about a product that a salesperson can't overcome, the salesperson at least will outweigh the negative comment with enough positive benefits to appeal to the prospect.

In any event, pressure won't work. This is the method favored by amateurs. They become defensive when an objection is raised. Unfortunately, objections often mean the prospect's defenses are up, too. When two defensive people are involved in any conversation (especially one relating to sales), very little communication is going to take place. No communication, no sale.

Of course, when an objection is stated, you can't always determine instantly whether it's an objection or a stall. Here is a very effective method I use to separate objections from stalls while preparing the prospect for the objection-handling process. Let's examine the procedure.

a. *Qualify the objection.* If the prospect hesitates to buy, he or she obviously has a reason. Ask what it is. This step won't be necessary, of course, if the prospect volunteers the reason, such as "The price is too high."

b. *Empathize with the prospect.* A fine way to get the prospect to lower his or her defenses is not to argue with the objection. Empathize instead or arguing. For example, you might say, "I can appreciate how you feel about high prices." Don't agree with the objection; just empathize with it.

c. *Feed back the objection.* This is the verification step. Restate the objection to the prospect to make sure you understand it. This also shows the prospect you've been listening. You might say, "To make sure I understand you right, you feel that the price is more than the value of the product, right?" Also, this gives you time to think of an appropriate answer.

d. *Isolate the objection.*   At this point, you don't really know whether the stated reason is an objection or a stall. Isolate the objection by asking an "if" or a direct question. For example, "If we can work out the price problem, would you be ready to buy?" Or you might ask, "Is price the only reason that makes you hesitant to buy?" If price is the only problem, then you have an objection. On the other hand, if the prospect hesitates to give you an affirmative answer to either question, then you will know that the prospect has handed you a stall—a smokescreen to cover the real reason he or she doesn't want to buy. You'll have to uncover the hidden objection. More on this coming up.

By following this process, you can keep prospects from becoming defensive and put them at ease while you overcome their objections.

There is bad news when it comes to objections. There is no single way to deal with them every time. But there is also good news. Most of them are so common that it's relatively easy to memorize the ways you deal with each one.

Don't Let the "Nos" Get You Down

Acting in the prospect's best interests does not mean quitting on the first no he or she might offer. Sometimes, people don't know that they want something until a successful salesperson has helped them realize their desires. Successful salespeople must believe in what they are selling. If they don't think that their products or services can truly benefit their prospects, either through profit, convenience, or both, then they should either find new products or find a new profession.

There are all kinds of reasons a prospect might refuse to buy. Here are seven common reasons I have come across.

1. *For the challenge.*   A seasoned buyer who has more experience than the salesperson might enjoy making the salesperson earn his or her commission. A salesperson who accepts this answer without at least trying to get the prospect to reconsider forfeits not only the sale, but also any chance of gaining the buyer's respect. Hang in there with the experienced buyer. Demonstrate your belief in what you are selling, and you might just change the no to a yes.

2. *For a lack of interest.*   You won't sell anything to someone who isn't interested. For whatever reason, the salesperson has failed to help the prospect realize a desire for the product or service. Keep selling. If feasible, perhaps a repeat of key elements of your demonstration would help.

3. *For the time being.*   Procrastinating buyers can be frustrating. They can't make decisions, so—like most procrastinators—they decide not to decide. They know they can always buy later. The salesperson who wants to make a sale today will have to change the prospect's mind. That's no easy task. You can pressure a procrastinator to make a buying decision, but more than likely you will get a decision not to buy. On the other hand, if you are too easy on the prospect, he or she will continue to procrastinate. The successful salesperson must be kind, yet serious, when giving strong, positive reasons for buying immediately.

4. *For no good reason.*   Such buyers often are criticized by others for not taking things seriously. They certainly could be so criticized by salespeople, because they have a penchant for turning them down. On the brighter side, they rarely hold to their decisions if the salespeople respond appropriately. Change the subject

to small talk, a joke, or an amusing anecdote. Then return to the sales presentation and ask for the order again. After a pleasant departure from the sales process, the prospect might be more willing to buy.

5. *For the sake of stubbornness.* Some salespeople can be perceived as being pushy by prospects who resent being told what to do. The salesperson shouldn't push a stubborn prospect. Instead, he or she must lead the prospect to an affirmative buying decision in such a way that the prospect will think it was his or her decision all along. Handle stubborn prospects with kid gloves.

6. *For the wrong reason.* An error in judgment or a misunderstanding on the prospect's part can lead to a fast no that can become a firm one if the salesperson clarifies the problem in a manner that embarrasses the prospect. Ask questions to determine precisely what the prospect misunderstands. Then gingerly review the sales process and product benefits, and carefully clarify what misunderstandings you have uncovered. Allow the buyer to save face, and you might save the sale.

7. *For a chance to get even.* Salespeople sometimes can be perceived as being pompous by prospects who feel inferior to them. And, of course, there might be good reason for this when a salesperson is truly pompous. Saying no at a salesperson's expense helps these prospects build their self-esteem and inflict a degree of revenge on their offender. Remember, customers provide you with income, so treat them as if they sign your paycheck. After all, they do!

Of course, there is always the chance that a no might actually mean no. Sometimes, prospects have very good reasons for not buying. These are called conditions. Some examples of conditions include no money, not being old enough to buy the product, or having no need or desire for it. What separates amateurs from pros is knowing the difference between conditions and objections. And although a refusal to buy might sound like a condition, successful salespeople always dig deeper to confirm it.

For example: If a person from a lawn care operation calls to entice a prospect to subscribe to the service, the prospect may say that he is selling his house. If the salesperson is an amateur; he might respond by saying, "Sorry I bothered you." A pro would say, "Great! I'm sure you're interested in attracting more prospects for your house. Let me explain how I might be able to help your house have better curb appeal." And then the pro would keep on selling.

Successful salespeople know when to give up for the time being, but it's not after the first refusal. They always try to find the real reason the prospect doesn't buy to prepare for the future with that particular prospect and to improve their selling ability. Furthermore, they always come back to try again.

Overcoming Logical Objections

Fortunately, most objections are used so widely that successful salespeople have found specific ways to deal with them. Perhaps they are used so widely because they are logical objections that often prevent people from making buying decisions. Let's take a look at the most common objections—the four reasons why people don't buy: no money, no desire, no urgency, and no confidence—and a method for handling each of them.

1. *The prospect thinks the price is too high.* When a prospect says the price is too high, it really means that he or she isn't convinced that the product is worth the asking price. The salesperson will then have two options: lower the price or build more value. Amateurs cut price, while professionals cut through such resistance by heightening their prospects' desires. For example, I would say: "Mr. Prospect, I think you'll agree that the cost of any product is directly related to the

savings that the product offers you. An investment in our product will produce savings that will more than justify its purchase."

2. *The prospect doesn't need the product.*   Remember, no one needs anything that he or she doesn't want. When prospects say they don't need a product, they actually mean they don't want it. Again, my response would be to heighten the prospect's desire by building value.

3. *The prospect is in no hurry to buy.*   This may be true. However, if you let it go at that, the prospect might buy later—but from another salesperson. When prospects delay, try to give them a bona fide reason for acting now—the best time to make a sale. For example, when prospects say they want to think about the decision for a while, I would respond by saying, "Fine, Mr. Prospect. Any questions you'd like to have answered? I believe I can answer them right now." (If appropriate, you can also use the following line: "I can offer you a free trial period at no obligation.") When prospects say they might buy later, my response is, "Later may be too late to qualify for this current price. First, there is inflation. And second, I can't guarantee that this low price will still be in effect at a later date. Why not avoid paying more by purchasing now?" When using this approach, be certain there isn't a hidden objection. Techniques on that coming up!

4. *The prospect has no confidence in the product, salesperson, or company.*   If the lack of confidence is in the company, it might be a good idea to arrange communication or a meeting between the prospect and company management. I have also used a client list here. Sometimes, the prospects have confidence in the clients you serve, or they might recognize friends who use your products or services. If the no confidence issue involves the product, perhaps a trial demonstra-

tion or a minimum order might satisfy the prospect's doubts. If the lack of confidence involves you as a salesperson, try to get the prospect to discuss candidly his or her reservations. Whatever the case, the no confidence objection must be overcome before you can close a sale.

Learn and understand these four most common reasons for no sale, and you'll have an effective weapon for dealing with most objections. When you overcome objections, verify every agreement and resolved objection with the customer to move closer to the sale.

The Hidden Objection

As I pointed out earlier, you might have to cut through several stalls to reach the hidden objection. Objections often are covered by stalls because the prospect doesn't care to explain the real objections for various reasons, including ego, self-doubt, lack of nerve (especially with the no confidence objection), or company-imposed restrictions that the buyer doesn't care to detail. Nevertheless, if you want to make the sale, you must discover and overcome the real problem. If you insist on fighting a smoke screen, you'll spend a lot of effort trying to perform the impossible.

When it becomes clear that the buyer has handed you a stall, probe for the real objection. I use this question: "Obviously, there is some reason you hesitate, may I ask what it is?"

If you have a very strong hunch as to the reason the prospect won't buy, play it. Although some prospects find it difficult to express their true objections, they might be likely to agree to statements that accurately assess their reservations, especially if the objection deals with a lack of confidence or a desire to compare competitive prices. Of course, you wouldn't want to give the prospect any ideas, but if you feel fairly certain about the hidden objection, sound it in question form. You might find the answer you need to make the sale.

Just remember to follow the process for clarifying the objection and putting the prospect in a proper frame of mind for you to handle it. A prospect who is kept from becoming defensive has a good chance of becoming a customer. Cutting through stalls and handling objections is the way to make it happen.

And when you've done that, the only thing left to do is close the sale. In the last chapter of this section I will show you how to close effectively.

Chapter in Review

1. A stall is the prospect's stated reason for not buying, while an objection is the real reason.

2. Early stalls include "I'm not interested," "I buy from a friend," "I'm satisfied with our present supplier," "I'm already using a competitive product," "I can't buy everything," and "Business is bad."

3. Actually, objections are prospects' positive contributions to the sales process. First, objections keep them talking, and second, objections keep the prospects' attentions focused on the product.

4. Handling an objection includes qualifying it, empathizing with the prospect, feeding back the objection, isolating the objection, then overcoming it.

5. A prospect might say no for various reasons, including for the challenge, because of a lack of interest in the product, for the time being, for no good reason, for the sake of stubbornness, for the wrong reason, and for a chance to get even with a seemingly superior salesperson. Successful salespeople are willing to persist beyond several nos.

6. The most common objections deal with the four rea-

sons people don't buy—no money, no desire, no urgency and no confidence.

7. Sometimes, prospects will stall rather than state their true objections. Successful salespeople must cut through the stalls to find the hidden objection.

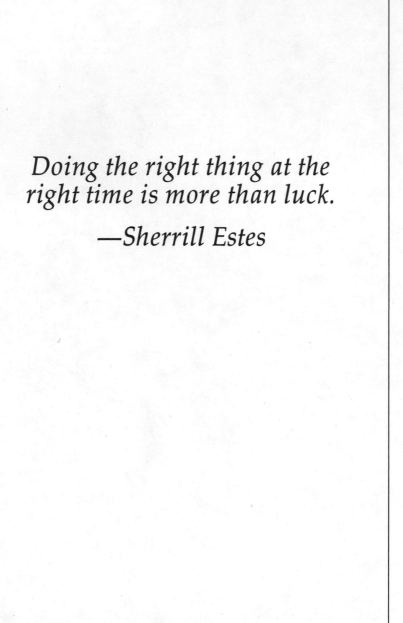

Doing the right thing at the right time is more than luck.

—Sherrill Estes

10

Closing: Ways to Persuade Them to the Finish

What happens to the young man who asks a girl to marry him on their first date? Most often, he gets rejected and the girl may never go out with him again. The young man's problem stems from the fact that he tried too early to close the sale.

Yet, if the guy plays his cards right, he will keep dating her until a marriage proposal might not seem like such a bad idea to her. By taking his time, he might eventually sell what he is proposing—matrimony.

Closing is not difficult. All it takes to close is to ask for the order. But knowing *when* to close can be a real problem. If you close too early, you're likely to be rejected, just like the young man with marriage on his mind. If you close too late, however, you run the risk of your prospect losing interest.

The secret to closing sales is do it at the right time—when the customer is ready to buy. And that's really not hard at all, provided you know what to look for.

Don't Turn Off

Our marriage-minded friend can be compared to the overly anxious salesperson who tries to close the sale thirty seconds after walking through the door. The prospect is likely to think the sales-

141

person is pushy, and rightfully so. Like the man in a hurry to get married, the salesperson is trying to make the sale without taking the necessary steps, not the least of which is getting the prospect to like him or her.

Such salespeople turn off their prospects before they get a chance to turn them on. On the other hand, there are salespeople who are willing to carry out each step of the sales process with precision and skill. However, they're unwilling to take the last step—to ask for the order—because they fear rejection!

What these salespeople don't seem to realize is that refusing to close produces the same result as being rejected. True, perhaps they can walk away with their egos intact, satisfied with the thought that, at least, they weren't rejected. But you can't spend an ego. Furthermore, a steady lack of sales can cause a salesperson to starve to death, and if that happens, he or she won't have any ego to feed! Besides, when prospects say no, they are not rejecting you—it's your business proposal they are rejecting.

Watch the Prospect

Sometimes, prospects will volunteer that they're ready to buy. Occasionally, when the salesperson has done a good job building value and heightening desire, the prospect will ask for the agreement and a pen. Most of the time, however, this won't happen. Yet, successful salespeople know when the prospect is ready to buy. Although the prospect might not put it in so many words, the skillful salesperson knows just the same, because he or she watches the prospect for buying signals.

Buying signals are nothing more than indicators of the prospect's interest in the product or service. Body language plays an important part in selling. While prospects often guard their words to conceal their true feelings, they sometimes aren't aware that their bodies give them away.

Of course, I could write another book on body language, but here are three major areas I watch closely to read the prospect.

1. *Facial animation or change.*   The crows feet on the outside of the eyes tend to become more pronounced with delight, anger, or concern. How can you tell the difference? Aside from judging the expression against the context of the situation, I also watch for the telltale smile or frown.

2. *The hands.*   You can determine a great deal about what a prospect is thinking by watching his or her hands. They might change position or activity. For example, drumming fingers might suddenly become still, or clasped hands might suddenly part. This transition actually tells more than the original action or position. A fine example of interest is displayed when the prospect picks up the sample product and starts to examine it.

3. *Significant muscle change.*   A prospect who leans back in his or her chair might be aloof. However, if the prospect suddenly leans forward, it's likely that he or she is interested. Arms and legs also can indicate the development of interest. Crossed limbs tend to indicate defensiveness, while arms unfolded or legs uncrossed tend to indicate openness.

Of course, none of these indicators is necessarily an absolute signal of interest. However, when weighed against the overall situation, they can serve to add weight to your own assessment of the situation. Being observant of body language certainly can help you determine when a prospect is ready to buy. The presence of such buying signals can help you identify the prospect's growing tension as he or she approaches a buying decision and the release of tension when the prospect has decided favorably.

Reading Between the Lines

A prospect can tell you that he or she is ready to buy in words that the average person wouldn't necessarily notice. For example, suppose a prospect asked one of the following questions:

- What colors are available?
- Do you arrange for financing?
- Is it difficult to operate?
- Could I get it by the first of the month?

To the average person, these might seem like questions that merely call for more information. And, of course, they do call for more information. But would the prospect ask such questions at all if he or she weren't interested in buying? If you were shopping for a car and saw a model that didn't appeal to you at all, you probably couldn't care less about its colors, financing, degree of difficulty to operate, or when you could get it, because you wouldn't want it in the first place.

When prospects ask such questions, a good salesperson can assume that they have assumed a mental attitude of ownership. And that's a good sign, indeed.

The Trial Close

The secret to staying in the sales profession is knowing when and how to close. Yet, even successful salespeople aren't always certain about when is the best time to close with particular prospects. So they stay successful because they're willing to make a closing attempt that is neither pushy nor presumptuous—a trial close.

A trial close is a marvelous tool for a salesperson who feels—but isn't entirely certain—that it's time to close. The beauty of a trial close is that, if the prospect isn't ready to buy, the salesperson has a comfortable retreat to the selling process at whatever point would be most appropriate.

A trial close is nothing more than an open-ended question calling for an opinion. "How does that sound to you, Mr. Prospect?" is a trial close that calls for an opinion. So is "What's your opinion of this product?" Of course, if the prospect responds by saying something like, "It sounds pretty complicated to me," or "I don't think I know enough about the product to form an opinion," the salesperson can simply resume selling by continuing to heighten the prospect's desire. This should be a comfortable transition, since the salesperson never actually asked for the order.

Open-ended questions are best for trial closes, because they call for elaboration from the prospect. Closed-ended questions, such as "Do you like the product?" or "I think this product will serve you well, don't you?" will only give you a yes or a no answer. A trial close is not the time to pin a prospect down to a specific course of action.

Some well-intentioned salespeople ruin perfectly good trial closes by tacking on to them a closed-ended question. For example, "What is your opinion of the overall plan, Mr. Prospect? Do you like it?" The second question closed what would have been a great open-ended question. Remember, keep your trial closes open for best response.

When dealing with a group of prospects, you might find that one prospect might pose a trial close question to another interested person. For example, a prospect might turn to his partner and ask a strongly leading question followed by a trial close, such as "I like this idea, Tom. How do you feel about it?" Sometimes, the prospect may ask only a trial close question, such as "Barbara, what do you think?"

When this happens, be quiet and listen. Don't help Tom or Barbara with their answers. At worst, you'll find what still has to be sold and to whom. At best, you'll get at least one order, and possibly more.

Don't Miss the Meaning Behind the Words

Of course, there is always the meaning behind the words, which might say something entirely different than just the words themselves. Suppose you were to ask a prospect, "What are your ideas about this product's appearance?" The prospect responds by saying, "It's okay."

That simple two-word answer, delivered without excitement, probably means that the prospect thinks there is something wrong with it. After all, if someone asked you to describe your spouse, you wouldn't respond by saying that he or she "is okay" unless you had some reservations.

Sometimes, the excitement or lack of excitement with which a message is delivered means as much or more than the actual words themselves. Always listen between the lines to make sure that you hear the meaning as well as the words.

There's More Than One Way to Close a Sale

Sometimes, prospects will remain indecisive about your product. Buying decisions are sometimes tough, and they become increasingly difficult as the cost of the product rises. As a result, prospects may put you off.

Of course, if you leave at this point, you run the risk of the prospect actually buying later—from another, better salesperson who could convince the person to act immediately.

Remember, if you truly believe in your product or service and its value for the customer, then you have an obligation to urge the customer to buy immediately.

That's the purpose of closing sales—not to pressure prospects into buying, but to help them make rational decisions to buy. And if you're a professional salesperson, you are simply acting out of conviction, because professional salespeople know that buying their products is rational. To sell a product that you thought was not worth the money would be second-rate selling.

Of course, just as there are many different ways to handle objections, there are a variety of closes from which salespeople can choose. Here are ten effective closes I use.

1. *The "Weighing" Close.*   This close is often called the "big ticket" close. There will be occasions when a trial

close gets a favorable response, but the prospect simply can't or won't commit to a decision. This close calls for the salesperson to help the prospect make up his or her mind by weighing the negative reasons for buying against the positive.

With a pencil and paper, list first all the prospect's reasons for not buying. If you did an effective job of listening, you should know what they are. Listing the negative reasons first should relieve any pressure the prospect might feel. When you're finished, get the prospect's agreement that there are no more negative reasons by asking, "I think these are all of the important reasons that might cause you to hesitate, aren't they?"

Assuming the prospect agrees, then list the positive reasons for buying—all the benefits pertaining to the individual prospect. Remember, prospects don't care about benefits of no significance to them. Keep the prospect involved in the presentation, getting his or her agreement with each benefit you list. The prospect might even volunteer benefits that didn't surface in the sales interview. If so, by all means list them. When you're finished, the positive reasons should outweigh the negative reasons, and you can conclude with a trial close, such as, "How does this look to you, Mr. Prospect?" If the answer is encouraging, ask for the order with a soft statement, such as "We can nail down that production date with your okay here." Then, hand the prospect the agreement and a pen.

The weighing close is not a miracle close, but I use it for prospects who have trouble making a decision. It will not overcome a poor sales presentation, and it will not cause a person to make a decision he or she feels is wrong. You might still get a put-off. If so, set a time in the not too distant future for a return visit—the next day, if possible.

2. *The "Forced Choice" Close.*   If a prospect is considering a purchase strongly but is hesitating to commit, the forced choice (or "alternative") close can be effective. The concept behind this close is to get the prospect to commit to a buying decision by agreeing to the terms of the sale instead of the sale itself. For example, "Would you prefer delivery on the fifteenth or the thirtieth?" His decision is based on his choice and not the product. This makes decision-making easier for some prospects. A word of caution: This type of close can backfire with prospects who do not trust you and who place a great deal of importance on feeling that they and they alone make buying decisions without help from salespeople. Be aware of the nature of your prospect. Be sure the bond of trust between you and the prospect is strong.

3. *The "Assumption" Close.*   With this close, the buyer assumes that the prospect will buy by asking questions like, "How soon do you want this?" or "How many of these do you want?" Again, make sure the bond of trust is strong when using this close. If it isn't, you might get an answer like never or none, respectively.

4. *The "Series of Decisions" Close.*   Remember, it's easier for the prospect to say yes to a buying decision if he or she has said yes to a series of previous questions. If my prospect has trouble making a buying decision, I would recap the major benefits in question form. For example, "We've agreed that the product will save you money, haven't we?" and "We've agreed that the product will pay for itself within six months, isn't that right?" By answering a series of questions designed to be answered affirmatively, the prospect will be more inclined to answer yes to the question "Then it would seem that buying is the rational and logical action, wouldn't you agree?"

5. *The "Go Ahead and Sell" Close.*   With this close, the salesperson takes an action (such as filling out an order blank) that will lead to a sale unless the prospect offers active resistance. Of course, should the prospect actually protest such action, the salesperson has an easy out by saying, "Don't be concerned. Unless or until you okay it, it's simply a worksheet for me." And you can put the prospect at ease by showing him or her where a signature is required before a sale can be closed. Of course, the beauty of this close is that it allows for a fast finish if and when the prospect decides to purchase. The key to this tactic is that the salesperson must have a great deal of poise and self-confidence. (By the way, as a reminder, salespeople never use the word sign when asking for a signature. Instead, ask for the okay. And it's not a contract. Instead, it's paperwork or an agreement.

6. *The "Don't Delay" Close.*   Some prospects can be motivated to purchase if the salesperson gives them a good reason not to delay. For example, "If you delay a purchase, I can't guarantee that the price will be the same. Add to that the reality of inflation, and you might pay considerably more money than you would now." If a prospect likes a product that is likely to undergo a model change in the near future, the salesperson might use the upcoming change as a persuading tactic.

7. *The "List of Satisfied Customers" Close.*   Some prospects can be influenced to buy if they know of others in similar situations who have been satisfied with their purchases. This is where testimonial letters can come in handy. Ask your customers for them, so you can use them to help you sell to others.

8. *The "Buy Now and You Get This" Close.*   If the buyer is postponing a decision, offer him a benefit for acting now. This tactic is often used in television selling of

products that aren't advertised elsewhere, such as
record albums and kitchen knife sets. The basis for this
approach recognizes that everyone likes something for
nothing, and the chance to get it might inspire some
prospects to buy immediately. Just make sure that
what you offer is of value to the prospect; an eight-by-
ten photograph of President Chester Alan Arthur
probably won't work.

9. *The "Objection" Close.*   As I pointed out in the previous chapter, an objection should be isolated to determine that it is, in fact, the only objection standing in
   the way of a sale. Once the objection is overcome, the
   only thing left to do is close.

10. *The "Ask for the Order" Close.*   All closes ask for the
    order in one way or another. But with this close, you
    simply and directly ask for the order. "Shall we go
    ahead with this?" or "Can I wrap this up for you?" can
    be most effective under certain circumstances.

These are my most effective methods for closing sales. You'll
take note that none of them called for begging. Professional
salespeople don't beg for orders. They provide products that are
equal to or greater in value than the prices they charge. They perform a service; they don't ask for charity.

Learn to close sales adeptly. Your success as a salesperson depends upon it.

And that closes our section on sales. But don't close the book.
We've got another section to go. This one deals with self-
management, and we'll kick it off with a chapter on goal setting.
Salespeople who understand the significance of goals often find
themselves much more motivated to sell!

Chapter in Review

1. The key to selling is closing at the right time—when the customer is ready to buy.

2. Buying signals are physical or verbal indicators signifying the prospect's interest in the product or service.

3. A trial close is an open-ended question calling for an opinion of the product or service. It's a marvelous tool because it allows the salesperson a comfortable retreat to the selling process if the prospect isn't ready to buy.

4. The purpose of closing sales is to help the prospect make the rational decision to buy. Successful salespeople know many different ways to close sales.

Part IV:
How to Manage Yourself for Sales Success

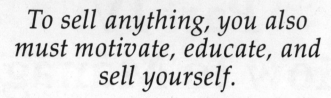

To sell anything, you also must motivate, educate, and sell yourself.

—Sherrill Estes

11

How to Be a
Super Salesperson

Why does anyone in a selling society sell anything, whether it be a product or service, an idea or relationship? Obviously, it's to gain a result that they believe will be to their advantage. They are motivated to sell by keeping in mind their own desires.

These outcomes may differ in nature. They can be the gaining of cash to pay the rent, a client who will generate a series of sales to provide security, support for a cause, or a relationship of mutual benefit, just to mention a few.

Although such outcomes vary, they can be classified under one term: goals. Goals are what keep salespeople selling, regardless of what they sell. And that's important to note, because professional, consultive salespeople know that true success is multifaceted. They strive to be successful salespeople not only when selling their products or services, but also during their off hours as well.

Side Effects of Goals

Goals do more than just give you a significant end to achieve. When you take into consideration all of the benefits that goals can produce, it's difficult to understand why only an estimated 3 percent of all people take the time and trouble to set them.

Goals make you a super salesperson. Let's look at the benefits of setting goals.

1. *Goals minimize the tendency to procrastinate.*   When a person sets a goal and realizes that he or she will reach it only through his or her efforts, the tendency to procrastinate is decreased significantly. It may disappear altogether. Only the people who plan to improve someday are the ones who find procrastination as attractive as it is easy to practice.

2. *Goals help you separate the important from the trivial.*   Carefully thought out and planned goals represent what is important to a person. As a result, the person with goals is in a better position to resist the temptation to do things that don't produce positive results.

3. *Goals save time and money.*   With careful planning people can save time and money, because they will know exactly how much time and money is available to them and how to get the most mileage from all their resources. The person who doesn't plan often wastes most of his or her resources.

4. *Goals give you cause for celebration.*   There are few better feelings than the one you'll experience upon achieving a goal. The more significant the goal, the more hearty the celebration.

5. *Goals can teach you.*   Goals can be great teachers. As you do the things necessary to achieve them, you can learn a lot along the way. Goals are also exceptionally good teachers when you fail to achieve them. Most failings offer lessons that, if heeded, will significantly reduce the chance of failure the next time a goal is undertaken.

6. *Goals help you concentrate.*   Since goals are based on rewards, goals will help you focus your abilities and resist any activity or practice that might jeopardize

your chances of reaching them. As they say, "Keep your eye on the prize!"

7. *Goals build your self-confidence.*   Reaching a significant goal can make your self-confidence soar. By accomplishing the goal, you will realize that you have the ability to succeed. This awareness will pay off in rich benefits later.

These are seven good reasons for setting goals in addition to the main reason—getting what you want. Perhaps you know of more reasons. Any reason you have for setting goals is a good one. Whatever inspires you to excel is a good reason. Use it!

Avoid One-Dimensional Success

Someone once said that the biggest failure in the world is the person who achieves success in only one area of life. 'Tis sad, but true.

Think about it. Don't you feel sorry for people who develop their bodies at the expense of their brains, and vice versa? Don't you hurt for the person who has gained a fortune but lost everyone he or she held dear in the process? The way to avoid such a shallow fate is to set goals in every area of your life.

We've already established how all people sell to others in one way or another. However, goals are nothing more than desires that people sell to themselves. Setting goals is the practice of self-selling, so to speak.

By selling yourself on the result you want to achieve, you can buy your way to a better life, provided you're willing to pay the price. To show you what I mean, let me compare the life situations of two people:

Jack wants to become a sales manager. He works toward the goal by reading and learning about what a sales manager does. To strengthen that knowledge, he takes classes to help him understand items like profit and loss statements, developing people, training functions, and setting objectives. He obtains a degree in business. He

also goes the extra mile that makes him successful by
achieving the goals set for him by his company or supervisor. Jack does all he can to make his supervisor look
good. He also takes advantage of every opportunity that
comes his way to prove his knowledge, even when this
may conflict with his personal activities. He does this
even when some would think he isn't getting adequate
pay for doing these things. Jack tries to involve himself
in learning every facet of the company by watching and
learning what other people are doing. Jack provides the
company with creative ideas that generate revenues. He
has good judgment and is imaginative. He has an action
plan for his goal.

Sounds like Jack has it all together, doesn't it? Let's compare him
with Bill, who also wants to be a sales manager:

Bill does not have the goal of becoming a sales manager;
he only wishes it would happen. He does his job very
well, but he doesn't take advantage of training classes or
making contacts with company superiors. He would
rather go home at the end of the day and relax. Bill
thinks eight hours is plenty of time to give to his company. He believes his boss doesn't offer him sufficient
opportunities to use his knowledge. Bill doesn't care for
Jack. In fact, he thinks of him as a "boot licker," and Bill
isn't about to lick any boots. It probably won't be long
before Bill decides he wants to work for someone else
because everyone in his department is getting promoted
except him. He blames his boss, the company, its products, and/or his coworkers. Too many times, his work is
so boring that he doesn't feel challenged.

Which person do you think has the better chance of being promoted? Obviously, it's Jack. Do you know why? Contrary to what
Bill believes, it's not because Jack is a "boot licker," which, for the
record, I don't think he is. Companies are full of sycophants (a
more scholarly term for boot lickers or yes men) who remain sycophants throughout their careers.

Jack will get ahead for one reason only: He makes it happen! He doesn't wait for a promotion to start learning the job. If he did, he would be like the person who waits for a car to run before filling it with gas. As we both know, things don't work that way.

Jack is the type of person who knows that the car must have gas before it will take him where he wants to go. He also knows that he won't get promoted until he is in a position to handle the increased responsibility. As a result, he takes responsibility for preparing himself adequately for promotion by setting goals. In short, he makes it happen.

Making It Happen

You, too, can make it happen by setting goals. Let's look at the various areas of your life where goals would be appropriate.

1. *Physical.* It isn't necessary to have a perfect physique to sell. However, if you've been in the field for any length of time, you'll agree with me that selling requires a great deal of energy. Aside from the fact that your schedule might require a great deal of moving about, it also takes energy to engage in the sales process. For those reasons, salespeople should stay in prime physical shape. Such a goal would be admirable, since negligence in this area could threaten other areas of life if not your actual life itself.

   How much does such a goal cost? It can be bought with proper diet, regular exercise, and adequate rest.

2. *Mental.* It isn't necessary to be a genius to sell, but salespeople can't be dummies, either. Successful salespeople are fast thinkers because they learn all they can about their products and the industries they serve.

   How much does this goal cost? Commitment to frequent study. Being a pro means that you are always learning.

3. *Financial.*   While money as a prime incentive often leads to burnout, it would be foolish to pretend that it isn't important. To get everything they want out of life, successful salespeople must set financial goals.

    To buy this goal, a person must invest specified amounts of money on a regular basis. And if you've ever had too much month left at the end of your paycheck, you'll know this is easier said than done. It's not impossible, however, and goals can help you immensely.

4. *Career.*   Of course, financial goals are going to be difficult to achieve without forming meaningful career goals that will motivate you to obtain necessary funding. Such goals might include a higher-level employment and/or landing certain lucrative sales accounts.

    The price for this goal is the willingness to develop and practice necessary skills.

5. *Recreation.*   All work and no play is no way to spend life. Although work is most important to a meaningful existence, recreation is the spice that provides enjoyable respite from day-to-day activities and, thus, helps people avoid burnout.

    The price to pay for this one? Aside from accumulating any necessary funding, you must be willing to set aside time to enjoy yourself. You definitely can afford this one.

Of course, you really can't afford not to pay the other prices if you want to become and remain successful. Success is truly multidimensional. Be willing to pay the prices. Look at them as investments, because they are. By conscientiously setting and pursuing meaningful goals, you will get returns that far exceed your expended efforts.

Setting Goals

When setting goals, use the following three guidelines to determine whether your goals are worthy of pursuing.

1. *Realistic.* Being realistic is not merely dreaming about being successful. You can reach for the stars all you'd like, but without a step-by-step action plan, you'll remain empty-handed. To get to the top of the stairs, you must take the steps leading to it. The same is true for getting to the top of anything else; you must take the proper steps. Therefore, if you're starting out as a salesperson, setting a goal to be president of the company in one year probably would not be realistic.

2. *Challenging.* The goal must be challenging; that is, it must be within your reach, but it also must cause you to stretch a bit. A person who made 100 sales per year would not be challenged by a goal to increase his or her production by 1 percent; such a goal could be obtained too easily. Likewise, a goal to double production within a year's time wouldn't be realistic because it would be too challenging, and the person would virtually be guaranteed to fail. Such a result could be so damaging to the person's self-confidence and self-esteem that he or she might have been better off not having set any goals at all. A successful goal challenges the person to perform a given task a little better than before. For example, while a goal to increase production by 100 percent per year probably would be overly challenging, a four-year goal to double production might be very realistic and challenging. That way the person would have four one-year goals to increase production by about 20 percent each year.

3. *Worthwhile.*   This simply means that the reward you
   receive will be worth your effort. It might be more
   money to do the things you enjoy, send your child to
   a better school, buy better clothes or a better car, go
   on a vacation, belong to an elite club, or build a savings account. It might mean recognition for your accomplishment, winning an award that earns you
   respect from others and yourself. It might improve
   your standing so that your opinion is sought when
   company policy is discussed. It might be getting a
   free trip for winning a sales contest, or a big promotion you've long desired. It might be a new title or
   more responsibilities. Worthwhile means the benefit
   you receive will be worth all the blood, sweat, and
   tears it takes to attain it. Therefore, before you attain
   it, the promise of the reward will be sufficient to
   keep you motivated to withstand any pain and sacrifices you must make to achieve it.

   If your goal isn't realistic, you're bound to fail. If it isn't challenging, you're bound to lose interest. If it isn't worthwhile, why
bother? Make sure that your goals have these three characteris-
tics to ensure your best chances of success.

Write Your Own Ticket

Wouldn't it be nice if we could write our own tickets in life? We
can write our own tickets by setting goals.

Goals are like road maps. With maps, a traveler can get from
point A to point B with little or no difficulty, because the map
shows exactly how to get there. Goals should be the same way.
They should be broken down into action steps that, when taken,
will lead to the desired result.

Suppose you were to bake bread. You wouldn't get bread from
the oven without first mixing the specified amounts of the
proper ingredients. Likewise, goals must be equally detailed and

properly measured before success can be achieved. For example, if you fail to measure all the ingredients in a receipe, what you'll pull from the oven will be a disaster, a failure instead of a success. You will have wasted the time and energy spent pursuing your goal, and you will likely be discouraged from trying again.

Back in my early career days as a salesperson I, too, didn't have the good judgment I have today. I believe it comes with experience and listening to those who have had more experience. As a rookie, I spent many hours out in the field making so many sales calls that I wasn't always timely in following up. I sent out a lot of untargeted letters and experienced tremendous rejection when I did follow up. I drove my car from one side of town to the other and came up short time and time again. I was about to become one of the statistics that I speak about; that is, one of the 90 percent who leave the field of selling frustrated and burned out. I had lofty ideas and big dreams and was not afraid of hard work, but mostly what I was lacking was a plan of action. I thought it was the number of calls that would produce the revenues to make me successful. Since then, I've learned that it's not so much the number but the quality of those calls. One of my early experiences, the turning point, was when our sales manager asked us to write on the back of a business card how much money we wanted to earn that year. Fearful that this was a "thinking big" quiz, we all wrote down large numbers. Then he asked us how many presentations we would have to make to generate our projected earnings. I don't believe any of us in that room really knew the answer. I learned that controlling the small things that we do each and every day is a secret to long-term success. In other words, if we use our time wisely and measure a goal, we are on the way to greater success. And, of course, knowing where you're going and how you will get there is the quickest way to success.

When you measure a goal, you'll know exactly how to obtain it. If you make 120 sales per year and you want to increase your production by 20 percent, you obviously must make 24 more sales per year. By measuring, you'll know that you must make an average of two additional sales per month to achieve your goal.

To make those two extra sales, you'll know that you must make a certain number of additional sales calls, depending on your calls-to-sales ratio.

Measuring Makes the Difference

By measuring goals, you won't feel as if you're pursuing the impossible dream. A person who wants to lose twenty-five pounds in a year might feel that the task is impossible and, thus, might succumb to the desire to overeat. After all, how much harm can just one more piece of cake do?

However, when the goal is broken down over a year's time, the person will have fifty-two weekly goals of losing about a half-pound. Such a goal isn't at all impossible, but it's not necessarily an easy feat. Thus, it's realistic, challenging, and worthwhile.

For this reason, it's a good idea to measure all goals by breaking them down into reasonable time elements and determining just how much you must accomplish during those periods to achieve your overall goal. Breaking your goals down into bite-sized tasks will make them easier to reach.

Plan Your Life with Goals

You can set a direction for your life by setting goals. The process involved is like the measuring process, except on a larger scale. Instead of breaking relatively small goals into bite-sized pieces, you can set large goals and break them down accordingly. Let me explain.

1. *Long-range goals.*   These are goals you'd like to accomplish within five to ten years. They might include saving money to make a significant down payment on a home, or being promoted to a prestigious company position, for example.

2. *Intermediate goals.*   These are goals that will lead to your long-term goals. Intermediate goals should take

between one and three years to achieve. Such goals might include setting a new sales record or completing studies that might lead to a degree.

3. *Short-term goals.* These are goals that should take from three months to a year. Increasing your production, getting into physical shape, or saving money for a vacation might fall into this category.

For maximum effectiveness, set goals in all three categories that pertain to each area of your life. In so doing, you'll make the most of your life.

Hints for Success

I've found that people pursuing challenging goals need all the help they can get. When setting goals, there are several things you can do that will help assure your success.

1. *Write down your goals.* Like the old Chinese proverb states, "The palest ink is more durable than the strongest memory." Then write down why your goal is realistic, why it is challenging, and why it is worthwhile. These will serve as reminders for you. Also, writing down your goals is sort of like entering into a contract with yourself. It can give you added incentive to succeed.

2. *Read your goals every morning and evening.* Review your goals regularly so you can assess where you are in relation to your destination much like a traveler consults a road map to find out how much farther he or she has to travel. By constantly reminding yourself of where you're heading, you'll be less likely to stray from the designated route.

3. *Believe you will attain your goal.* This is a critical step. Several old adages apply here: "Whether you believe

you can or cannot, you are always right." "Winners expect to win. Life is a self-fulfilling prophecy." "Nobody will believe in you unless you believe in yourself first." Belief in one's self is essential to the goal-setting process.

4. *Announce your goals to your friends and associates.* This will give you added incentive to achieve them, because you won't want your friends to think you can't succeed. Don't worry if your associates laugh at your goal (your friends won't). You can have the last laugh (and the best one) by succeeding.

5. *Create a support system.* Develop a group of people who will help see you through the sacrifices it takes to obtain your goals. This group might include your spouse, children, friends, and your clergyman. Goals require sacrifice. Expect them, and be prepared to handle them. It's always easier to endure disappointments when you have friends and loved ones to help you through them.

6. *Form good habits and drop bad ones.* Make a list of practices that will move you closer to your goal and resolve to follow them. By the same token, make a list of bad habits that will move you farther away from your goal and resolve to avoid them. As it has been said, "Bad habits are easy to form and hard to live with. Good habits are hard to form and easy to live with." Good habits lead to success, while bad habits often lead to failure.

7. *As soon as you reach one goal, set another.* You wouldn't quit your job just because you broke a company sales record. If you're a super salesperson, you'd set another goal to surpass it. Without challenges life would be meaningless.

When you know where you are going, how you are going to get there, and the length of time it will take, your odds of reaching your destination are increased significantly.

Even if you fail, you'll be a lot closer to your destination and a much more effective person than you would have been otherwise. Furthermore, you'll be in a better position to try again.

Yes, goals are truly the motivation behind being a super salesperson. If you haven't done so already, start setting some goals of your own. The advantage you'll gain will be tremendous.

As a salesperson constantly having to meet the monthly quota deadline, I learned I could do it through setting goals. Doing it all and getting it all done was another chore. Being a mother, wife, consultant, speaker, and businesswoman is a busy life. Let me share with you how to do it all in the next chapter.

Chapter in Review

1. Goals are what make you a super salesperson.

2. Goals offer positive side effects that will contribute to a salesperson's self-development.

3. One-dimensional success is not success at all. Salespeople should set goals in every area of their lives.

4. Goals should be realistic, worthwhile, and challenging.

5. Goals should be broken down into action steps to clarify what actions are necessary to achieve them.

6. Salespeople should set three different types of goals: short-term, intermediate, and long-range.

7. For best results, goals should be written down and read frequently. A person setting goals should believe that he or she will achieve them, and announce their goals to their friends and associates. Goal-setters should create a support system of friends, form good habits and drop bad ones, and set bigger goals when they achieve their original ones.

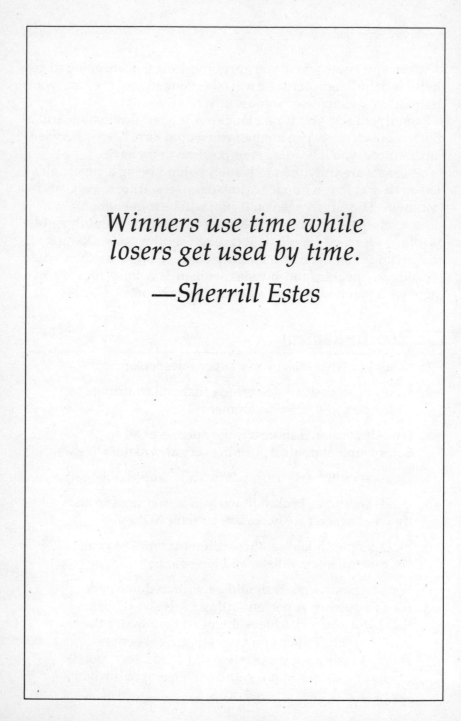

*Winners use time while
losers get used by time.*

—Sherrill Estes

12

Doing It All and Getting It Done

T ime is running out!

Even as you read these words, your life clock is ticking. However long or short that may be, we'll have to do our best with the time that we have. And unlike money, everyone has the same amount of time in each day—royalty and paupers alike.

What makes the difference is how we use it.

There is a bright side to this law of time. Just as your volume of time past slowly but surely increases to the point of significance, so, too, will your production, if you approach it on the same basis. Rather than spending your time trying to land the sale to end all sales, you'll profit much more easily (and quickly) by learning to bite off just a little more responsibility every day—gradually—until one day, you'll have quite an income.

Time is what separates winners from losers. Winners know how to use time to their best advantage, because they develop good time habits that offer significant positive results over the long haul. Losers often are the products of poor time habits, which also can offer significant consequences—but not the kind you'll want to live with.

You can't add more time to your days. But by developing good time habits, you can add more effectiveness to your efforts and more dollars to your income. And that certainly will go a long way toward helping you better enjoy the time you have left.

Time Management = Goal Setting

The previous chapter on goal setting should have given you all the information you need to manage yourself properly. After all, time management is nothing more than goal setting—on a very short-term basis. If you can set goals that you want to accomplish in three months to five years, certainly you can set goals that you can achieve in a day. That's the concept behind time management.

By setting daily goals that are realistic, challenging, and worthwhile, you can increase your production significantly over a period of time. For example, if you are able to make one additional sales call per working day, you will have reached 260 additional prospects in a year's time. Even with a sales ratio of ten calls to one sale, you still will have made an additional twenty-six sales at the end of the year. What would you have done with the commissions if you had made twenty-six extra sales last year? How about next year?

You can let your major goals take care of themselves by practicing good time habits. Just as a weakling working with weights doesn't become muscular in a week, a salesperson also must be willing to spend some time developing and practicing these habits to boost his or her income.

Avoid Time Traps

An important part of setting good time habits is avoiding bad ones. Many well-intentioned people frequently stumble into time traps, or situations that take time they could be using for productive activity.

Much of my success has come from avoiding the following time traps.

1. *Lack of planning.* Are you a star rep? This is the rep who covers all points but who misses areas in between because of a lack of planning. He or she starts from the office and drives out to the north end of town for the first appointment, then cold calls or canvasses the south end before keeping an appointment in the east

end. After that, it's back to the office early because it's too late to get to the west end before quitting time.

Lack of planning is the most common time trap of all. Too many salespeople fail to plan, and some of them discover they might as well have planned to fail. Others avoid planning because they are relatively successful without it. However, thoughtful planning not only can mean the difference between failure and success, it can mean the difference between success and greater success. Who doesn't have room in their lives for more success? Sure, planning takes time that you could be using for selling. But if you're smart, you'll plan during your off time and save your prime time for making money.

2. *No clear priorities.*   When salespeople aren't aware of their most important objectives, how can they hope to succeed? Again, it just goes to show how planning can make the difference.

Are you a flounder person or a trout person? A flounder lies on the sea floor, waiting for food to come its way. Its movements are controlled by tides, and it doesn't resist natural forces. As a result, it can be caught easily. But a trout swims against currents, chooses its food carefully, decides when to resist and when to rest, and is very difficult to catch.

Likewise, flounder people react only to what comes their way. They wait for things to happen and concentrate on activities. Trout people act with forethought and self-discipline. They make things happen and concentrate on goals and objectives.

The difference between the two? Priorities!

3. *Overcommitment.*   If you commit yourself to do things that will take up more time than you have at your disposal, you're bound to reach the end of the day with unfinished work. Learn to say no when necessary. If you're too busy to handle incoming calls for a co-

worker, say so. If you can't do something for a prospect or client by a certain deadline, don't commit yourself. It's better to disappoint people with refusals than
to commit yourself and leave them in a tough spot
later because you weren't able to come through.

People who overcommit their time get bad reputations, much like people who overcommit themselves financially get bad credit ratings. When a
person becomes notorious for not keeping commitments, his or her general effectiveness is bound to
suffer. Commit yourself only when you know you
can keep your commitment.

4. *Indecision.*   Some salespeople find it difficult to
make decisions. They might fear the consequences of
erroneous judgment, or they might refuse to decide
until getting all of the facts—some of which might
not be forthcoming for a long time, if ever. And some
seem to lack the ability to make rational decisions.
Meanwhile, the clock keeps ticking. All a person can
do is get all the available facts, weigh the negatives
against the positives, and then decide. Be successful
by being decisive.

Don't be like the fellow who went to the grocery
store to buy breakfast cereal. He couldn't decide which
kind to buy, so he settled for an assortment of cereals
packaged in small, individual serving boxes. But at
breakfast the next day, the man faced more trouble because he couldn't decide which cereal to eat.

5. *Meetings.*   An attorney once told me of a criminal de-
fendant's case that went to deliberation. She was encouraged by the fact the jury had been out for about
two hours until she learned that the jurors had only
been haggling over who would serve as foreman. Once
that issue was decided, the jury convicted the defen-
dant in less than thirty minutes. The moral of this
story? Sometimes, minor issues can take more time to

settle than major ones. Some meetings are necessary, some are not, and virtually all of them last too long, thanks to everyone's desire to be heard.

When possible, make decisions without meetings, and discourage unnecessary meetings.

6. *Telephone.* The telephone is a good tool that can save a lot of travel time for salespeople who want to check on certain accounts. However, it can eat up a lot of productive time for salespeople who don't know how to use it effectively. Screen all incoming calls and group your outgoing calls so they can be made at one time.

7. *Socializing.* In a business environment, it's only natural that some people will enjoy each other's company. There is nothing wrong with that—provided the socializing doesn't occur during time that you could be selling. Enjoy friendships over lunch or after hours.

Any one of these traps might not take a great deal of time, but when several are added together, you'll find yourself wondering where your day has gone. Perhaps the best time habit you can start is to avoid these time traps.

Win with Good Time Habits

You will notice measurable results when you take active time-management measures. Let me give you a dozen helpful tips I use.

1. *Make a "to do" list.* This will help you operate with clear priorities. At the end of each day, make a list of the most important tasks facing you the next working day. Then, rank them in order of importance. First thing the next morning, tackle task number one and complete it before moving on to task number two.

Complete that task before moving to number three, and so on.

Charles Schwab, past president of Bethlehem Steel Company, spent five minutes at the end of each afternoon preparing a "to do" list for the next day. He said learning the value of the list was "the most practical lesson I've ever learned." Schwab was made a believer by results. He had been putting off a call to a particular client for nine months. He decided to make it number one priority for the next day. As a result of the call, Schwab landed a $2 million order!

2. *Schedule your time.*   Put yourself on a schedule. Allow plenty of time for your sales calls and responsibilities. This will combat any tendency to overextend yourself. Also, it will help you separate what is important from what isn't.

3. *Get organized*!   A lack of organization can waste a lot of valuable time. The minutes fly by while you shuffle through papers to find a particular document or needlessly retrace your steps. Organize your briefcase, your desk, your car, your home and office, and have a designated place for everything.

4. *Organize your presentations.*   You'll save not only your time, but your face as well, by taking this step. Salespeople who stumble and stutter because they haven't prepared sufficiently waste not only their time (and the prospect's time), but also a good opportunity to make a sale. Remember, prospects seldom buy from unimpressive salespeople. Furthermore, know your prospects and customers well, so that you won't budget time for C and D customers at the expense of A and B buyers.

5. *Don't waste travel time.*   When long distance or heavy traffic driving is necessary, critique your last sales presentation, or mentally organize your next one. Take along a cassette player (if your car doesn't have one) and listen to an instructional or motivational tape. If you're taking a bus, train, or plane, have worthwhile material to read, or do your paperwork.

6. *Avoid procrastination.*   Many people delay doing what is necessary because they dread the task or lack the self-confidence to proceed. If a dreaded task must be done, get it out of the way. You'll feel better when it's behind you. The way to develop the self-confidence to perform a necessary task is to go ahead and do it. Of course, if the task isn't necessary or worthwhile at all, then you probably should forget it. In any event, don't procrastinate with important tasks. It usually will cost you money, plus a lot more time when you finally get around to doing it.

7. *Preserve your prime time.*   Don't schedule nonproductive tasks during your prime time. Whenever your prospects are most commonly available is the time to be selling. Doing anything else will cost you money. Save your paperwork for a Saturday or some other time, such as evening or early morning.

8. *Be flexible.*   Even the best laid plans are likely to go awry from time to time. Build flexibility into your schedule. If an appointment is delayed, have some reading material available. If you know the delay will be lengthy, politely inform the receptionist that you'll make another appointment, then pursue another productive task. This would be a good time to make cold calls or spontaneous, unannounced visits to new prospects. Be guided by your schedule, but don't be a slave to it.

9. *Make appointments that are mutually convenient.* The best appointments are those set for a time and place that suit both you and your prospect.

10. *Allow for the unexpected.* When scheduling time for a particular task or an appointment, always try to reserve a little extra. Delays beyond your control have a way of occurring. However, a salesperson late for an appointment won't score any points with the prospect, regardless of his or her reason. If all goes well and you arrive early, you can spend the extra time preparing your presentation.

11. *Work from the outside in.* Salespeople who start working their territories from the central office to the boundaries often find themselves failing to call on distant accounts because they have the temptation to call it quits too early to beat the traffic back to the office and wrap up the day. Salespeople who start at the boundaries and work their way toward their offices solve the traffic problems and make their calls, too.

12. *Get up an hour earlier.* If you're accustomed to sleeping until the latest possible time, try getting up an hour earlier. This would be a good time to do paperwork or read material that can help you strengthen your skills. Not only will you be better able to meet the demands of the day by rising earlier, but you'll also add 260 hours to your work year. Divide that by eight (the number of hours in a work day), and you will have added more than thirty work days to your year.

The following table will help you determine the value of your time and how much saving it can be worth to you: It is based on 244 eight-hour work days (excluding breaks).

ANNUAL INCOME	EACH HOUR IS WORTH	EACH MINUTE IS WORTH	AN HOUR A DAY FOR A YEAR IS WORTH
$25,000	$12.81	.2135	$3,125
$30,000	$15.37	.2561	$3,750
$35,000	$17.93	.2988	$4,375
$40,000	$20.64	.3440	$5,036
$50,000	$25.62	.4270	$6,250
$75,000	$38.42	.6403	$9,375
$100,000	$51.22	.8536	$12,499

Although you can't really add hours to your day, you most certainly can add productive hours by decreasing the amount of non-productive time you spend. These twelve good time habits will help you be more productive.

Tips to Keep You Going

Even by adding productive time to your schedule, you still must have the energy to meet the demands of the day. Here are some tips that will help you make the most of the time you have.

1. *Get plenty of rest.*   Salespeople need plenty of energy to meet the demands of selling. One way to maintain a high level of energy is by getting plenty of rest. All people, especially active ones, need sleep to rejuvenate themselves. Also, a lack of proper rest will show itself in yawns and bleary eyes, which are very unbecoming to professional salespeople.

2. *Exercise regularly.*   Do you know that a physically fit person can get by with less sleep than a person who is out of shape? A physically fit person also will feel better and have more energy. If you can devote thirty minutes just three times a week to some form of exer-

cise, you'll find that the benefits will make it more
than worth your while.

3. *Understand the law of inertia.*   The law of inertia states
   that an object in motion tends to stay in motion, while
   an object at rest tends to stay at rest. One reason many
   salespeople feel like dropping in their tracks at the end
   of a day is because they have taken too many breaks.
   An automobile will burn more fuel by starting and
   stopping frequently than one that runs continuously.
   By the same token, it will take less energy for a salesperson to get started and keep going than it will if he
   or she takes frequent breaks.

4. *Set high goals.*   Super salesperson Frank Bettger said
   that he got more done by working four and a half days
   on a tight schedule than by working constantly with
   spaced-out sales appointments. Aside from letting the
   law of inertia work for him, he probably got additional
   energy from setting high goals. With the goal of accomplishing more than an average day's work, plus
   the reward of an extra half-day to tack onto a week-
   end, it's no wonder he was energetic. You'll develop
   extra energy, too, by setting high goals.

5. *Provide regular maintenance for your car.*   Flat tires and
   car breakdowns can happen to anyone. However, the
   odds of it happening to you will increase if maintenance is neglected. Wouldn't it be a waste to miss a
   sale that could contribute hundreds of dollars to your
   income because of a flat tire?

You can't be productive if you can't keep going. Make sure that
you're not grounded at a time when you need to be flying by following these practices, as well as the previously mentioned productive time savers. When you're making the best use of your time,

you'll find that success will grab you before you have a chance to recognize it.

Furthermore, you'll find it easier to keep a positive attitude about your profession, which is essential for successful selling. However, there's no law that says you can't develop a positive attitude about your profession from the start. The final chapter of this book explains what type of attitude a professional salesperson should have to succeed.

Chapter in Review

1. Time is what separates winners from losers. Winners know how to use time to their best advantage, because they develop good time habits that offer significant positive results. Losers often are the products of poor time habits.

2. Time management is nothing more than goal setting on a very short-term basis.

3. Avoid time traps such as lack of planning, lack of priorities, overcommitment, indecision, unnecessary meetings, inefficient use of telephone, and socializing during selling time.

4. Add productive hours to your day by making a "to do" list, scheduling your time, getting organized, organizing your presentations, making the best use of travel time, avoiding procrastination, preserving your prime time, being flexible, making mutually convenient appointments, allowing for the unexpected, working your territory from the outside in, and getting up an hour earlier.

5. Keep yourself going by getting plenty of rest, exercising regularly, working with the law of inertia, setting high goals, and keeping your car in good condition.

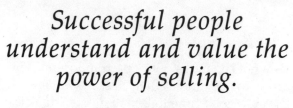

*Successful people
understand and value the
power of selling.*

—Sherrill Estes

13

Motivating Yourself to Great Success

Although I have sold my way to success, I am not the first person to say we live in a selling society. The concept is probably as old as time itself. And I believe that one reason so many salespeople fail is that they don't understand fully *all* the selling involved in professional selling.

Professional sales is more than just trading a product or service for money. As I've pointed out, a professional salesperson must sell desire, confidence, benefits, and value, not to mention himself or herself, too. That's a lot of selling!

Many salespeople aren't even aware of how much selling is necessary to make a sale and, therefore, they haven't the faintest idea how to begin.

I don't want to give the impression that the job of selling is easy, because it certainly isn't. The failure rate will attest to that. But I most certainly want to give the impression that the profession is rewarding, because it is—if you do it correctly.

The preceding twelve chapters have been devoted to teaching you the proper techniques that will equip you to succeed. However, this last chapter is the key to it all. The information in it will help you develop or strengthen the one vital quality it will take to use effectively the skills you have learned.

That one crucial quality is called attitude. No matter how well-versed on techniques a salesperson might be, it will mean absolutely nothing without the proper attitude. Instruction is fine, provided it can be applied to the real world.

After all, many people can play basketball; they know the techniques. But only skilled players have developed the proper attitude that enables them to win an NCAA Championship. It's the positive attitude that makes a winner.

By the same token, successful consultive salespeople have the right attitude. They know that to be successful they must help others get what they want. Therefore, they are truly interested in the prospects and are willing to listen, ask questions, and recommend a product or service that will best suit the prospect's desires.

A salesperson's attitude very often, if not always, is the trait that allows him or her to apply knowledge effectively and efficiently—provided the attitude is in good shape. If it isn't, the salesperson will be fighting (and probably eventually will lose) a battle that will be uphill all the way. The following people share the belief that attitude is of overwhelming importance.

- The difference between a successful person and others is not a lack of strength, not lack of knowledge, but rather in a lack of will.—Vincent T. Lombardi
- He who believes is strong; he who doubts is weak. Strong convictions precede great actions.—J. F. Clarke
- You will become as small as your controlling desire, as great as your dominant aspiration.—James Allen
- It is a funny thing about life; if you refuse to accept anything but the best, you very often get it.—W. Somerset Maugham

A person's attitude can indeed be powerful, be it positive or negative. Prisons and mental institutions are full of people whose destinies were determined by actions borne out of negative attitudes. On the other hand, the world has many stories about people who overcame hardships to become successful. Obviously, their actions were motivated by positive attitudes.

Fortunately, attitudes are developed, not inherited. That means that no matter what attitude you have now, it can be changed or strengthened. If you want to take responsibility for your success, acquire a positive attitude if you lack one, and take care of your positive attitude if you have one.

Attitude—The Only Freedom You'll Never Lose

Noted psychologist Victor Frankl was a prisoner in a German concentration camp during World War II. He survived the ordeal and recorded his experiences and observations. He noted that prisoners fell into three categories.

The first group consisted of people who were motivated by anger. They tended to lash out by attacking the guards, and, most often, they were killed on the spot.

The second group contained people who were motivated by self-pity. Resigned to the inevitability of death, they died spiritually, in a sense. They were prone to focus on their own misfortunes, constantly weeping and lamenting. Most of them eventually died, too.

The third group was made up of survivors—the ones who accepted the reality of their situation and tried to make the best of it. They didn't focus on themselves as much as they did on others. They were quick to help those in need and comfort those overcome with sorrow.

The third group had what the others didn't—a realistic and positive attitude. And, in the end, that's what made the difference between death and survival.

Frankl also observed that the difference in attitudes was the result of personal choice. He noted that the one indestructible human freedom is a person's ability to choose his or her attitude. Although all other freedoms can be taken away, the ability to choose an attitude remains with us forever.

Successful salespeople choose to operate with positive attitudes. Not only are positive attitudes more productive, they also cause less distress.

What a Bad Attitude Can Do for You

You've probably known people with negative attitudes. They're afraid to take risks, because they lack the self-confidence to succeed. Therefore, they never progress. They often worry about a mistake in the past or dread a fearsome future event. In so doing, they become too preoccupied with themselves to recognize—let alone, benefit from—opportunities and pleasures that might come their way. Bearing this in mind, it's easy to understand why people with bad attitudes often don't succeed.

If they only chose to have good attitudes instead, life could be different. They could develop the self-confidence to succeed, rationally weigh risks against rewards, and proceed accordingly. They would realize that worrying is wasted energy that contributes nothing positive to their present lives. They wouldn't worry about mistakes; instead, they would learn from them, for all mistakes offer lessons that can be valuable to a person's development. They wouldn't worry about future events; instead, they would prepare for them, for every future event offers a chance for preparation, which also can be valuable for a person's development.

Instead, they doubt and worry. Unfortunately, that's not the path to success in sales or anything else, but rather to a possible nervous breakdown.

No one should fear failure. It's a risk a person runs anytime he or she tries to succeed. The only person who can be 100 percent certain that he or she won't fail is the person who doesn't try. Unfortunately, that's also the only way to be 100 percent certain of avoiding success.

Don't be afraid to fail. As noted automaker Henry Ford once said, "Failure is the opportunity to begin again more intelligently." People learn from their failures, and Ford was one to know. He failed and went bankrupt five times before he succeeded as an automaker. Few people know that, because millions of cars in this nation bear his name.

People tend to forget a person's failures when he or she finally succeeds. Noted baseball player Babe Ruth held the record for the most home runs scored by a single player—751—for more than four decades after his death. Few people know that he also still holds the record for most strikeouts—1,330 of them.

Just be sure that when you try anything, you try it with a positive attitude. That often makes the difference between success and failure.

Development of a Positive Attitude

Even though I am used to closing million-dollar deals, I also have experienced much rejection along the way. Some days, rejection is inevitable, no matter how smart you are or how responsible your actions are. On those days, you have to think positively and put everything into perspective. One afternoon, many years ago, I had to pick up nine desktop dictating systems from a law office in a country town. This law office had just spent all of its money redecorating and renovating its old offices, so it could not afford the systems. As I walked down the stairs with several of these large boxes and a briefcase in my hand, in my high-heeled shoes, I stumbled and fell down the stairs. Everything fell out of my briefcase. Some of the equipment broke and my skirt was almost over my head. My knees were bleeding and my ego was bruised. Realizing that it was just part of the day and not all of it, I stood up, fixed my skirt, fluffed up my hair, picked up my equipment, and left. I promptly walked across the courtyard into another law office to introduce myself and my products. I made a very strong presentation, demonstrated many ways the prospect could cut costs and save time, and sold several systems that afternoon. Whenever there are bad moments, I try to look at the humor in the situations and simply realize that sometimes life is difficult. It's how much you let those things get you down that will determine your long-term success. Many novices would have cried and gone home or back to the office. But I believe in the silver lining. Keep on keeping on even when your legs don't want to!

So on tough days, here are some tips I use to keep my sanity and put negative feelings into perspective.

1. *Act positively.*   Psychologists have discovered that it's
   easier to act your way into feeling than it is to feel your
   way into acting. People who are depressed can cheer
   themselves up by acting happy. By the same token,
   this tactic works in reverse. Many attorneys feign
   anger to prove points in court and make impressions
   on juries. As a result, they find themselves actually
   angry. Use this practice to your advantage. When you
   don't feel very positive about a given situation, try to
   act positively. You probably will find that your attitude
   will change accordingly.

2. *Feed yourself positive thoughts.*   Don't focus on misfortunes and setbacks. Dwelling on a painful memory
   prevents you from attaining a healthy mental attitude.
   It's needlessly painful. When tempted to dwell on negative thoughts, try substituting positive ones instead.
   Sometimes, it's a matter of how you look at a situation.
   Don't punish yourself for blowing a sale. Instead, reassure yourself that it won't happen again, because you
   now know better.

3. *Expect to succeed.*   When you set goals, believe fully
   that you will be able to attain them. To believe otherwise would be decidedly negative, which could have a
   profoundly negative affect on the results you achieve.
   No matter what you undertake, genuinely believe that
   you can succeed, and expect it. It can have a most positive affect on your performance.

4. *Envision success.*   You can recharge your positive
   attitude occasionally by envisioning the success you
   seek. Periodically, envision yourself succeeding,
   and imagine the reactions of your peers and the rewards of your efforts. It's not only a great way to
   keep positive, but to keep your eye on your goal as

well and avoid any temptation to do things that
would be counterproductive.

5. *Seek out positive friends.*   According to the old
   adage, "If you run with dogs, you'll pick up fleas."
   It's true. People who associate frequently with negative people generally become negative themselves.
   On the other hand, people who seek the company
   of positive people usually have little trouble main-
   taining their positive attitudes. This is not to say
   that you can't have any negative friends, but it's not
   a good idea to live with them.

6. *Keep your perspective.*   Perspective is a positive
   attitude's best friend. Without perspective, the first
   setback or disappointment that comes along is
   likely to throw you into the depths of despair. Successful salespeople generally overcome most of
   their setbacks and disappointments through the
   power of perspective.

Positive attitudes are very powerful, but they require on-
going maintenance. Keep yours in shape with this six-step
process for building a positive attitude.

Spread Your Positive Attitude With Enthusiasm

If the best salespeople are those with positive attitudes,
wouldn't it stand to reason that the best prospects are those
who also have positive attitudes? Certainly! And the best way
to get a prospect thinking positively is by being enthusiastic
about what you do and what you sell.

As James M. Barrie said, "The secret of happiness is not in
doing what one likes, but in liking what one does." Enthusiasm
is not keeping a poker face or speaking in monotone. Enthusiasm is contagious. It's also the mark of a professional. After all,

if the salesperson can't get excited about his or her product or service, why should the prospect get excited?

Consultive salespeople must believe in the ability of their product or service to satisfy their prospects' desires. When salespeople are sold on the fact that they can offer benefits of equal or greater value than the prices their prospects must pay, they can't help but get excited about the win-win situations they have the ability to create.

Your enthusiasm perhaps will be your greatest source of power for engineering successful sales relationships. Don't keep it a secret.

Taking Care of You

Of course, enthusiasm alone won't sell products and services. That job is up to you, and how well you are able to do that in the future depends largely on how well you take care of yourself.

So let me end this book by offering you three pieces of advice that, if followed, will help you, too, to realize success in sales.

1. *Accept yourself.*   You are unique. There has never been, nor will there ever be, another like you. You have strengths and weaknesses, just like everyone else. Learn to position your uniqueness and abilities as assets. Confidence is more than 50 percent of the battle. A strong sense of self-esteem will allow you to march to the beat of your own drummer. In the 1970s, I noticed one thing about men and women in business—they all appeared to be conformists wearing blue suits, white shirts, and a little blue draw-string tie or bow tie. Everyone looked the same! We all had our battle uniforms, as I called them. However, as my career progressed, I realized that being a nonconformist could help me. Recently a lady noticed my pearl-colored hoisery. She said, "Sherrill, as women in business, don't you think that we shouldn't be wearing those?" I replied, "To

be quite honest with you, I think it's perfetly ac-
ceptable to be a women into business, be feminine,
and still be taken seriously. I believe that we have to
be nonconformists so that we can stand out." Therefore, instead of sending Christmas cards to my clients I send out Fourth of July cards or whatever else
I can think of that is imaginative and different. I
can get a lot more mileage out of my resources if I
march to the beat of my own drummer. I believe in
doing things differently.

I learned a very valuable lesson as a youngster
about the benefits of nonconforming and calculated
risk taking. My father owned a single-engine
Cessna and one Sunday afternoon he asked my
mother, my sister, and me if we would accompany
him on a trip in his airplane. On the way home, my
father looked over at me and asked if I would like to
learn how to fly the plane. I said, "Yes," and he
turned the controls over to me. As I dove in and out
of the clouds like a top gun, I looked over my shoul-
der and caught my mother's eye. She looked terri-
fied! Then, I glanced at my father and he had a
twinkling in his eyes, the look of the eccentric mav-
erick. He was totally delighted to teach me how to
fly the plane and to my mother's amazement we
did land without incident. I look back on that trip
and realize that we have to step out of the comfort
zone to succeed. You must have the confidence to
do things differently, but sometimes you just need
pure luck. Of course, I believe in taking calculated
risks and perhaps that wasn't the finest example of
a calculated risk. My father never took calculated
risks, he took big ones. But I find that most people
cannot take risks, even small, calculated ones. Living under his direction led me to be most comfortable with big calculated risks. Confidence and a
healthy perception of yourself are fundamental to

leading people, closing big deals, and achieving
great success.

2. *Judgment.*   If you want to develop a "big deal mentality," you must be disciplined enough to work long
   hours and make the most of them. If you run
   around all over town, spinning your wheels, writing
   letters, and not following up on the people you
   have called, you are just making noise and not exercising good judgment. Look for ways to simplify
   your systems and paperwork. Develop good habits
   and cut costs. But most of all, use time, don't get
   used by it.

3. *Think big.*   Much has been said about thinking big.
   That means having the self-confidence to go for the
   big deals. What is most important is imagination,
   the creativity to put together big deals. The imagination to get the most out of your day is the key to
   great financial rewards. Question everything, be
   imaginative, be thrifty with assets and time, and
   cultivate major accounts. If you can step back and
   evaluate the big picture you will find great success
   as a consultive salesperson.

   Remember, the secret to consultive selling is taking care of
your customers. I have just shared with you my secrets to
consultive selling. If you are wise and innovative you will have
the flexibility to protect your reputation and your customers.
Consultive selling is as much an attitude as it is techniques. It's
about integrity and having a strong sense of self-esteem and
confidence to help others succeed.
   Take care of yourself first by learning the techniques and developing a winning attitude, and you'll be in a prime position
to take care of your prospects and customers. When that happens, your financial rewards will follow; then, you will enjoy
the rewards of selling like a pro!

Chapter in Review

1. No matter how well-versed on techniques a sales-
    person might be, it will mean absolutely nothing
    without the proper attitude. A salesperson's atti-
    tude is often the trait that allows him or her to
    apply knowledge effectively and efficiently.

2. Attitude is the only freedom you'll never lose.

3. Lack of confidence and worrying have kept many
    people from succeeding. Successful salespeople
    have positive attitudes, which play a large role in
    building self-confidence and avoiding worry.

4. Don't fear failure. It's a risk a person runs any-
    time he or she tries to succeed. It also can be a
    good learning process that will help you learn
    how to succeed.

5. Build a positive attitude by acting positively,
    feeding yourself positive thoughts, expecting to
    succeed, envisioning success, seeking out positive
    friends, and keeping your perspective.

6. Enthusiasm is the mark of a professional; it's also a
    fine vehicle for spreading a positive attitude.

7. Take care of yourself by accepting yourself as a
    unique being, developing good judgment and
    thinking big.

FOR MORE INFORMATION ABOUT SHERRILL ESTES'
SEMINARS PLEASE CALL OR WRITE.

TRI S CORPORATION
P.O. BOX 563
CRESTWOOD, KENTUCKY 40014
(502) 241-4711

INDEX